WILD LIFE

IN

CANARA AND GANJAM

WILD LIFE

IN

CANARA AND GANJAM.

BY

GORDON S. FORBES

GYAN

Published by

GYAN

Gyan Publishing House
5, Ansari Road
Daryaganj, New Delhi-110002
Phone: 011-47034999, 9811692060
E-mail: books@gyanbooks.com

Distribution Network
gyanbooks.com
India, USA, Canada, UK, Australia

ISBN: 978-93-6208-105-6 (PB)
First Published, 1885

2nd Impression 2024

Printed at: Gyan Press, Delhi.

WILD LIFE IN CANARA AND GANJAM
Author: GORDON S. FORBES

ESTUARY OF GAIRSAPPA RIVER.

WILD LIFE

IN

CANARA AND GANJAM.

BY

GORDON S. FORBES,

Madras C. S. (Retired.)

LONDON:

SWAN SONNENSCHEIN & CO.,

PATERNOSTER SQUARE.

1885.

TO

The Dear and Honoured Memory

OF

SIR HENRY CONYNGHAM MONTGOMERY, BART.,

Late of the Madras Civil Service.

INTRODUCTION.

An author is only justified in offering to the public a record of trivial and unimportant matters when he can satisfy curiosity by telling of things and people not generally known, and scenes remote from the highways of the world.

I hope that my chapters of Indian experiences may be held to have this justification, and I would fain see descriptions, from the pens of those who know them well, of the many other little-known regions and races which are scattered up and down the far-extending dominion committed to English keeping. At present such narratives are rarely to be met with, though a few good specimens have recently appeared.

Only in this way can a true conception be given of the many varied aspects of life and nature to be found in the hill and forest tracts of India; her city populations and agricultural communities are better known, though much that is interesting remains untold, owing to the fatal barrier of caste, which shuts off the European from intimate acquaintance with Hindoo life.

My experience of Canara extended

from October, 1844, to near the close of 1848; and I served in Ganjam as collector, magistrate, and agent in the hill tracts from August, 1858, to September, 1867. The illustrations for the Canarese portion of my narrative have been supplied by my friends Mr. Ward and Mr. Ballard, the frontispiece being from a painting of Mr. Ballard's, taken from an original sketch of the falls of Gairsappa by another old friend, the late Mr. Charles Whittingham; the coast scenery is from very accurate drawings by Mr. Ward, and the encampment at Neelcoond is from a sketch of my own.

TABLE OF CONTENTS.

CHAPTER I.

Introductory.—Physical Features and Boundaries of Canara.—Mad Raja of Coorg.—His Cruelties and Whims.—Journey Northwards.—The Munchiel.—The Scenery.—Fishing at Condapoor.—Belikeri.—Its Bay.—Cove of Beitcole.—Isolation . *pp.* 1–15.

CHAPTER II.

The Sawuntwari Rising.—Its Temporary Success.—Our Precautions.—The Sheiksendies and Dessaies.—Uses of the Bayonet.—A Veteran of the Old School.—Progress of Operations.—Captain Tainton's Wager.—His Death.—The Forts.—Colonel Wallace's Operations.—The Elephant Rock—End of the Rising.—Teak Forest.—Ravine of the Kala Nuddee.—The Races of Soopah.—Origin of the Sidhis.—Katijah Beebe.—Breed of Buffaloes.—The Bull and the Tiger.—The Toucan . . . . . . *pp.* 16–38.

CHAPTER III.

Belikeri.—Laterite Cliff and its Caves.—Nux Vomica.—Wild Mangosteen.—Sea Otters.—Porcupines, and How to Trap Them.—Our Fishing Village.—Byroo and his Men.—Alligator.—Its Power of Ejecting Things Swallowed.—Little Nap.—Harpooning Fish.—The Great Saw-fish.—Manner of Feeding.—Pearl Oyster.—The Iguana.—José Prebhoo's Stories.—The Tigress Stops the Way.—Bear and Postal Runner.—A Fight with a Python.—Another Combat.—The Bluebottle and the Ants . . . . . *pp.* 39–62.

CHAPTER IV.

Honama and his Men.—Their Forest Cultivation.—Their Nets and Manner of Hunting.—Netting a Tiger.—Critical Moment.—Ancola and its Fort.—The Man-eater and its End.—

Another Leopard.—The Kill.—The Vital Point.—"Don't Shake his Tail."—A Fish in a Puddle.—"From Whence did it Come?"—Effect of Monsoon on Wild Animals.—A Hand-to-Hand Fight.—Man-eater near Sedasheghur.—He Mocks us.—Officer Killed near Hyderabad by a Tigress . *pp.* 63–83.

CHAPTER V.

Gokern—Pilgrim and Bear.—Propensity of Bears to Get at the Brain.—The Rocks of Yáana.—Wild Bees and their Prejudices.—The Bees and the Surveyors.—Approach to Yáana.—Its Appearance.—Difficulty of Explaining the History of the Rocks.—The Bison.—Its Appearance.—The Dorsal Ridge.—A Bull of Nineteen Hands.—Another Bull.—A Bison Stalk.—Another Encounter.—Invulnerability of the Head.—Manoel.—His Courage.—An Instance . . . . *pp.* 84–106.

CHAPTER VI.

Sirci.—A Naturalist and His Ways.—Bison's Power of Leaping.—Mr. Ward's Collections.—Bison Calf.—Flying Squirrel.—Approaches to Sirci.—The Cotton Trade.—The Carriers of India.—Their Services to the Country and to our Armies.—Encampment at Neelcoond.—Swimming the River.—Obstinacy of Cotton Traders.—The Falls of Gairsappa.—Approach through the Forest.—Novel Kind of Piers for Bridges.—Description of the Falls.—An Adventurous Seat.—Lines on the Cataracts . *pp.* 107–129.

CHAPTER VII.

Visit to the Haigah Brahmins.—Suicide or Murder?—Difficulties.—The Dug-out.—A Man of Action.—The Haigah Village.—Leeches.—My Lodgings.—Arica Gardens and Terraces. — The Cow-house. — Description of Arica Palm and Mode of Gathering Nuts.—The Monkeys.—Cardamoms.—Blossom and Manner of Cultivation in some Forests.—Spontaneous Generation . *pp.* 130–142.

CHAPTER VIII.

The Nilgherries. — Their General Aspect. — Climate.—Flowers.—Game.—Ibex.—A Buck before Breakfast. — Emerald Moss. — Toda

Buffaloes.—The Toda Race.—Landslip.—We Sight Ibex.—Doe and Kid.—The Buck.—The Elk and their Haunts.—A Stalk.—Rebellion among the Members.—We Lose the Stag.—My Friend's Stalk—Surprise.—A Tiger Stalks Him.—Wild Dogs.—Their Respect for the Domestic Dog.—My Meeting with Them.—Elephants.—Death of Mr. Wedderburn.—Mr. M.'s Meeting with a Rogue Elephant . . . *pp.* 143–169.

CHAPTER IX.

Ganjam.—Its Races.—Dispossession.—Ooriyah Zemindars.—Khonds and Sourahs.—Human Sacrifices.—Infanticide.—No Amalgamation of Races has Occurred.—No Affinity of Language.—Khonds Ignorant of Use of Milk.—Tobacco.—Weapons.—The Gond Potters.—The Bottle Gourd.—The Potter's Model.—My Duties in Ganjam.—Agency for the Hill Tracts.—Physical Conformation of the District. . . . *pp.* 170–180.

CHAPTER X.

The Chilka.—Its Origin and Extent.—Fish.—Birds.—Islands.—Birds' Eggs.—Inhabitants of Bird Island.—Young Herons and Pelicans.—Deer Island.—Antelope.—An Antelope Drive Extraordinary.—Trade of the Lake.—Oil-cake and Manure for Cane.—The Lake Boats . . . . *pp.* 181–192.

CHAPTER XI.

Rhumba.—The House.—Mr. S. and His Mode of Life.—His Administration.—What Became of his Accounts.—He Refuses to Quit.—Dismissal and Exposure. — Sale of Rhumba House.—Sequel of Mr. S.'s History.—Visitors.—Other Visitors at Midnight.—Dilemma. The Gipsy Shikaries.—Their Trained Antelopes.—Visit to the Antelope Grounds, and Capture of a Wild Buck.—Manner of Harnessing the Buck.—His Training.—Landrail's Nest.—Cobra and Rails.—Fox and Rails.—Alligator and Wild Duck.—Coast Lagoons and Canals . . *pp.* 193–212.

CHAPTER XII.

Chetterpur. — Abandonment of Ganjam.—The Tumpra. — Use of the Pandanus. — Fox Coursing.—Wolves.—Shepherd and Python.

—Other Snakes.—Bears and Sugar-cane.—Drawing a Bear.—Mr. Minchin Wounded by a Bear.—A Sentinel.—Mad Jackals.—Three of our People Bitten. — Stramonium a Cure for Hydrophobia. — Its Use by Thieves . . . . . *pp.* 213-230

CHAPTER XIII.

Mahendra.—Mystery of its Temples.—Ooriyah Ignorance about Them. — Legend of the Pándava Brothers.—Small Temple on the Summit.—Difficulty of Building it in Such a Place.—Other Temples and Grottos.—Interrupted Work.—Raja of Mundasá.—His Spirit and Perseverance.—Interviews with Two Young Officers.—Our Visit to Mahendra Appreciated. — Vassal Sourahs. — Independent Sourahs. — Cottage on Mahendra . . . . . *pp.* 231-242.

CHAPTER XIV.

The Khond Highlands.—Meria Sacrifice.—Kidnapped Victims.—Their Indulgent Treatment.—Manner of Sacrifice.—Discovery by Captain Macpherson.—Rescued Merias.—Recaptured by Khonds.—The Special Agency for Suppressing Meria under Colonel Campbell.—Force at his Disposal.—His Success and that of Captain MacNeil.—Attempt to Make an Agricultural Community of Rescued Merias.—Its Failure.—Limits of the Khond Country.—Survey Maps.—Khond Cultivation.—Full Dress.—Khond Trade.—Khond Tribal Combats. — My Work as Special Agent.—Change in the Character of the Force.—Police Patrol and Measures to Stop Infanticide.—Absence and Return to Ganjam, January, 1866.—Bad News.—Encounter of Police with Kootiya Khonds. — The Soorada Khonds.—Collisions with Them.—Simli.—Our Captives.—Submission of the Tribe. — Khond Women. — The Oath. — A Rattle.—Sal Trees.—The Famine.—"The Cry of the Land" . . *pp.* 243–270.

Wild Life in North Canara.

CHAPTER I.

INTRODUCTORY.

THE following chapters record some experiences of a residence in a wild and beautiful forest region, remote from the more civilized districts of southern India. The writer was charged with the revenue and magisterial administration of that portion of Canara which extends for about fifty miles along the borders of Goa and Belgaum, and found himself isolated from European surroundings, but in a position to see much of the unsophisticated races who lived and laboured in and around the great teak forests of North Canara, and of the wild animals which abound there.

In 1845 North and South Canara formed one great province, with a coast line of about two hundred and fifty miles, ending at the Portuguese frontier. On its eastern side the little kingdom of Coorg, the Mysore dominions, and the districts of Darwar and Belgaum covered a frontier of three hundred miles, at an average distance of fifty miles from the western coast; and of the entire area thus enclosed, by far the greater portion was hill and forest.

Before leaving Mangalore for my charge in the north, I heard from the then collector of Canara a singular episode in the career of the mad Rajah of the neighbouring state of Coorg, of which he had himself been an eyewitness.

The Government of India had for a long time vainly endeavoured by counsel and remonstrance to curb the cruel excesses of the tyrant of Coorg, and it became necessary at last to coerce and depose him; but before resorting to force a last attempt was made to bring him to reason by deputing Mr. Russell, a member of the Madras Government, who was personally known to the Rajah, to visit and advise him.

One day while Mr. Russell was urging the utter hopelessness of opposition to a power like that of the British Government, the Rajah turned to him and said, "I know, Russell Sahib, that your Government is powerful, but its commands are not obeyed as implicitly as mine are." "Here, you two," said he, calling two of his people, "climb up that cocoa-nut tree." Up went the men and looked round for orders before descending, "Let go, hands and feet!" The men instantly obeyed and were both killed by the fall. "Call the wives and children of these men," pursued the Rajah. The poor women appeared before him trembling but in silence. "What is this which has been done?" "The Rajah's good pleasure has been done," they answered. Then the murderer turned triumphantly to Mr. Russell.

On another occasion he questioned his visitor closely as to the person in whom the supreme power was vested in England, and was told that it was the Queen. "But you say," objected he, "that the Queen cannot do everything she might wish to do; who is above her?" "There is no one, only God is her superior," said Mr. Russell. "God! Please write that name down for me, that I may remember it." This was done, and the matter dropped. Mr. Russell returned unsuccessful to Madras, and troops were sent against the Rajah.

The Coorgs fought bravely for their tyrant, strong stockades defended the approaches to his capital, and these were only forced at the cost of many lives. The Rajah was then made prisoner, our troops occupied the town, and the officers were quartered in the palace, the largest hall in which was set apart for a mess-room.

Some surprise was excited when it was found that all round this hall, just under the cornice, were emblazoned the titles and name of the Rajah, and immediately below them the name of God, under which again appeared the name and title of the Queen of England. This was the madman's way of announcing his superiority to all other powers in heaven or in earth!

I started for the Bay of Belikeri, my head-quarters in North Canara, in the month of December, when a steady and continuous northerly wind renders sailing up the coast tedious. I therefore travelled by land in a munchil, a simple and ingenious contrivance peculiar to the western coast of India, and which merits special description.

A stout canvas hammock, the ends of which are prevented from collapsing by crossbars of wood let into the extremities of the canvas, is suspended by chains from a pole of nine or ten feet long. The chains are fastened to rings in the crossbars, and the hammock hangs about two feet below the pole; a thin mattress and a pillow complete its internal equipment, and the traveller is secured from sun and rain by a broad waterproof top which rests on the upper side of the pole, and can be slanted at will to either side. The munchil is very comfortable, and so light that four bearers easily run along with it at five miles an hour. My first night's run in this conveyance brought me all the way to Coondapoor, quite sixty miles north of Mangalore, the point from which I started.

Nothing more beautiful is to be seen anywhere in Europe or Asia than the coast of Canara. Mountain spurs from the main range of the Western Ghauts run down to the coast and sometimes extend far out to sea, wooded to the water's edge, and mapping out broad bays or landlocked coves; in other places they flank the estuaries of navigable rivers which come winding among the hills from the east, bordered—as the valleys open out and admit of cultivation—by plains of brilliant green. All this wealth of picturesque outline is bathed in the soft brilliancy of tropical atmosphere; and the effect, to eyes unfamiliar with the scene, is a happy stupor of admiration. Many a half-hour did I waste in helpless gazing, when I reached my future home at Belikeri, where the charms of the coast seem to culminate.

Coondapoor was a fair specimen of western coast scenery, but I am chiefly concerned to describe the curious sort of fishing I saw there.

There was in that neighbourhood, in the grounds of an ancient temple, a rectangular sheet of water of fifty or sixty yards wide; and in this pond were fish of a kind not to be found elsewhere, and quite unique in their habits, inasmuch as it was impossible to net them in the ordinary way, and they were to be caught, if caught at all, in the air and not in the water. The pond was preserved and the fish were seldom disturbed; but I was much pressed to attend and witness the process of netting them.

I found a canoe provided for me, and took my seat in it. But first of all about twelve men advanced into the water in line at intervals of ten feet or so, each holding upright before him, above the surface, a stout pole. From pole to pole along the line stretched a net of six or seven feet broad, so that as the fishermen proceeded to wade slowly right through the pond up to their chins in water, an upright net held above water moved with them. I followed behind the net in my canoe. When we had got more than half-way across, and were approaching the opposite bank, there rose suddenly from the water a numerous flight of large fish, most of which leaped clean over the six-foot screen of net, a few only sticking in the meshes. One fish fell in the canoe, and another leaped almost in my face. This went on until we got close to the bank, by which time the great majority of the shoal had cleared the net. The fish were very much of a size, being about fifteen inches long, with red-tinted fins, and of about the outlines of a four-pound barbel, but with a more pointed head. I was told that they were full of bones, and not otherwise good eating.

I have never seen or heard of anything like this very peculiar fishing elsewhere, nor can I understand why the fish did not escape between the men in the water, where there was nothing to stop them.

The leaping was a pretty and curious sight, the fish taking their fence like a set of trained hunters.

A second night's journey in the munchil brought me to Honore, the last station on Madras territory; and a third run of forty miles to Belikeri Bay.

I found the house there to be a spacious barn-like building on a laterite cliff about seventy feet above the sea, and standing in extensive grounds on a promontory which formed the southern shore of a bay worthy to challenge com-

BAY OF BELIKERI.

parison with the Bay of Naples. To the east, the north, and the north-west the hills rose like a camp round the broad blue circle. Towards the south-west shore there was an opening seaward of a mile and a half wide, exposing a portion of the bay to storms from that quarter.

A perfect and far-famed haven of refuge in such cases was however provided a little farther north, where another spur of the same range enfolded a lovely cove, called Beitcole, completely lapping it round from all the winds of heaven, and endearing its name to every mariner of western India.*

---

* A breakwater has since been added to these natural advantages, and the Port of Karwar created.

My house though spacious was absolutely empty, and within reach of its beautiful surroundings were to be found none of the ministers of civilization common at all Indian stations. Practically I was as remote as Robinson Crusoe himself from the doctor, the butcher, the baker, etc.

I sent therefore to Goa (about seventy miles north) for a family of carpenters and a flock of turkeys, and imported a flock of sheep from Mysore. Ancola, our nearest bazaar, furnished a sack of wheat and a hand-mill; the cook became the butcher, the tent lascars I taught to make bread, extemporising an oven. When the carpenters arrived they rapidly put together some furniture from the pretty yellow wood of the jack-tree, and thus the means of civilized life gradually grew and multiplied around us.

As the Sawuntwari insurrection was at that time disturbing our northern frontier near the Soopah tableland, which was a portion of my charge, it is necessary to explain what occurred and the precautions taken to protect our passes.

I was about to make the revenue settlement of Soopah for the year then commencing, and marched with my tents and official establishment to the upper country for that purpose, camping at Yellapore, a small town surrounded by forest, where were the head-quarters of the Tahsildar of Soopah. Arrived at this place, I set myself at once to understand our position and devise means of resistance if occasion should arise.

CHAPTER II.

THE SAWUNTWARI INSURRECTION.

SAWUNTWARI is a forest tract at the southern extremity of what is called the Southern Mahratta country, abutting on the Portuguese territory and on the province of Belgaum. It lies between the tableland and the sea, and is not far from the ghauts or wild passes which lead up from the lowlands to Soopah. Five such passes give access to the Soopah talook from Goa, and as many more ascend to Belgaum from thence, and from Sawuntwari;

and as all these hill roads cross the British frontier from foreign territory, there was in those days a little custom-house at the head of each pass for the levy of import dues.

What first brought Phond Sawunt and his clan into collision with our authorities I cannot say; but when I assumed charge of Soopah and Ancola the Sawunts had plundered and burnt the Belgaum custom-houses and committed sundry other acts of violence. Troops were sent out against them from Belgaum, but as so often happens, when regular troops are sent into the jungles to attack undisciplined enemies on their own ground, the latter had much the best of it, and our regiments lost men and officers without being able to close with their enemy. News of these encounters began to reach me soon after my arrival from the reports of frontier officials, both on our own and the Belgaum border, but I was not in communication with any higher authority possessing such information as would enable me to test the accuracy of these unpleasant tidings.

It was mortifying enough to hear them from native sources, and to find that my own establishment regarded my proposed progress through Soopah for the purposes of settlement as uncomfortably hazardous. Necessarily, both the country and the people were entirely new to me; but I had an excellent map, and I found myself well seconded by the district officials when once I had formed my plan for defending our passes, and got leave from my chief at Mangalore to carry it out.

I enlisted one hundred and fifty matchlock men in the forest villages lying along the crest of the Northern Ghauts,—men who were the descendants of feudal retainers of the Mahratta chiefs of old days,—keen shikaries, familiar with forest life, and priding themselves on the semi-military character of their associations. They were called sheiksendies, and a portion of them were employed as village constables under the potails, or heads of villages, whose forefathers during Mahratta rule had themselves been Dessaies, or petty chiefs. Probably Phond

Sawunt's levy consisted chiefly of a similar class of men; so that if our passes were invaded, Greek would meet Greek. Among the little custom-houses I distributed thirty peons armed with musket and bayonet and sword, and well provided with ammunition. These men were to be in constant communication with the sheiksendies, whose duty it was to patrol the border near the head of each pass and to keep up the communication. They were also instructed to rendezvous promptly under their Dessaies at any point which might be threatened.

When I put my thirty peons through their facings with musket and bayonet, a controversy arose among them as to the proper use of the bayonet, the prevailing opinion being that its manifest intention was to put out the eyes of the enemy, and that it ought to be directed accordingly. To settle this important matter, I pointed out as gravely as I could that all parts of an enemy's person were equally suitable for the application of the bayonet point! With the use of firearms both peons and sheiksendies were perfectly conversant.

Before starting on their beat, my hundred and fifty sheiksendies were paraded for inspection, wiry and strongly-built little men, each carrying a matchlock taller than himself, with powder-horn and pouch, and either a sword or wood knife. They wore a dress peculiar to that region, and which I have not seen elsewhere: a thick white cotton tunic reaching nearly to the knee, and very tight-fitting breeches of the same material, laced at the back of the calf. On the whole I was agreeably surprised at the appearance they presented drawn up in line, and I harangued them in Hindostani on their duties. Many of our Mahratta ryots in Soopah bore the name of Sawunt; and as I was rather apprehensive of sympathy being felt in Soopah for the cause of Phond Sawunt, I thought it necessary to impress on the Dessaies and their men that collusion or sympathy with rebels was as heinous a crime as rebellion itself. When my harangue was ended, old Motuppa Dessaie came forward and propounded a very pertinent question on a point I had omitted to notice. "Sahib," he said, "do you authorize us to shoot down these men if we see them in our jungles?"

My point of view having all along been that of resistance to attack, the question was new to my mind. I could not tell my men to shoot strangers at sight like deer, so I instructed them to call upon all comers from the hostile quarter to surrender, and to use their weapons only in case of resistance or attack.

These arrangements made, or rather while they were in progress, I ordered my people to prepare to carry out our tour of settlement exactly as had been proposed, and met with no further remonstrance from them. We had marched from Belikeri by way of the Arbyle Ghaut, and encamped at Yellapore, the chief town of Soopah. Here was located the office of the Tahsildar of Soopah, a grand old veteran who in early life had seen the Duke of Wellington when he passed through Hullial (an ancient town on the confines of Soopah), and who was conversant with the history of the Mysore and Mahratta campaigns. This old Brahmin was on the verge of life, but full of fire and energy, and, if need should arise, full of fight. I found him early one morning outside his cutcheri, carefully swathed against the cold, raw fogs of the season, but scrutinizing keenly, one by one, all the muskets of his armoury; a peon was proving before him the locks and flints of every weapon again and again. The old man's finely-cut face was of an extraordinary corpse-like pallor, but when he was animated his eyes blazed with a brilliancy strange to see, and I think he was quite disappointed that he was not called upon to stand a siege in his cutcheri. His known courage and energy, and his intimate knowledge of the people and country were of great service to me. He did not long survive that season, and I grieve that I cannot recall his name. Meanwhile the Sawuntwari disturbances continued, though they did not extend into Soopah. Troops were moved up toward the border. A regiment under General Lovell was posted at Sirci, about twenty miles from Yellapore. A detachment of four companies encamped at Hullial, a town on our western border, and Colonel Wallace on the Belgaum side was in command of a considerable force, including artillery.

Among the casualties which occurred in the early operations against Phond Sawunt, I remember particularly the death of Captain Tainton, a man who was reported to be the best shot and the best racquet player in southern India, and who was unrivalled in the skill with which he could use almost any kind of weapon. He once made a singular wager (which he won), to the effect that he would, with a pellet bow and a supply of the hard clay pellets used with it, prevent an antagonist placed face to face with him from loading and discharging a pistol. With an unceasing shower of pellets he proceeded to knock about the pistol, the powder flask, and the knuckles of his antagonist, till the latter had to give up attempting to load and confess himself beaten.

While leading his men through the jungles of Sawuntwari, Captain Tainton received his mortal wound from a matchlock ball. He carried a double-barrelled gun on his shoulder, and turning as the shot struck him, caught sight of the smoke of the matchlock in the bush, and shot the man dead just before he dropped himself.

The end of the rebellion did not come till two or three months later; but

Colonel Wallace pressed the Sawunts hard, and at last Phond Sawunt and his seven sons and a body of their retainers threw themselves into two forts so difficult of access that they were reported by the natives to be impregnable. One of the forts was called Munoghur, or "the fort of the heart," the other Munosuntosh, "the delight of the mind."

But Colonel Wallace at last destroyed the reputation of these maiden forts. He discovered that there was a secret way of approach from the foot of a precipice called the elephant rock, and having made his preparations, he one night lowered guns and men down the face of the precipice and marched upon Munoghur and Munosuntosh. The surprise was too much for the Sawunts, and they fled, leaving the forts empty and undefended. Phond Sawunt and his sons were captured in the Goa jungles not long afterwards, and imprisoned; and so ended the Sawuntwari rising.

The course of my official tour in Soopah made me acquainted with every part of it, and I found that almost the entire area was occupied by a vast forest, consisting in great part of valuable teak timber. A well-grown teak tree is a beautiful thing, the trunk is straight and shapely, ascending from forty to sixty feet without a branch; above this imposing shaft the limbs of the tree extend laterally in much the same proportions as those of the Scotch fir. The leaves of the teak tree are very large and of rather a light shade of green. This teak forest in some places extended over the brow of the ghauts, and stretched seawards, covering a part of Ancola. I could ride in one direction across my charge for forty miles in shade, except where village clearings intervened at distant intervals.

It will be clear to the reader that I am describing an exceptional region, and I will here mention some further features of the Soopah tableland. One of these was a profound ravine which crossed it diagonally from east to north-west, and completely cut it asunder, rendering all ordinary traffic impossible.

At the bottom of this ravine, and

nearly two thousand feet below the average level of the country, ran the Kala Nuddee, or black river, which as it left the limits of Soopah turned due west and reached the sea at Sedasheghur, not far from the boundary line between Canarese and Portuguese territory. Notwithstanding the great depth to which the river had furrowed the surface of the country, the ravine had not the nature or appearance of a cañon, the sides slopes, though very steep, were practicable for an active man, and were covered from top to bottom with lofty teak trees.*

---

* During a subsequent visit to Soopah I sent round my horses by the usual road, and followed this tract through the ravine and over the river. It proved rather an arduous walk, but a very

We used to send letters from Yellapore to the north-eastern part of Soopah across this ravine when the river was low, throwing bridges of rude temporary planking from rock to rock; but this was not possible when the river was full, and the usual road for the greater part of the year turned the head of the ravine by a *détour* which made the distance between forty and fifty miles instead of less than twenty.

The inhabitants of this singular tract were in some parts Mahrattas and in others of Canarese race, but there was a third and less numerous section, of

---

interesting one, the steep pathway wound among teak trees of great stature, with no underwood beneath them; an absolute solitude where the silence was unbroken.

pure African descent, called Sidhis. These men were descendants of fugitive slaves from the Portuguese settlement, who had found a secure and congenial home in the great Soopah forests, where they formed hamlets and villages, obtained and cultivated lands, and throve and multiplied. In appearance the Sidhis retained their ancestral type absolutely unchanged, and were the same ebony coloured, large limbed men as are still to be found on the African coast, with broad, good-humoured, grinning faces. At one time they were great smugglers, but when I knew Canara they had become loyal subjects and gave no trouble. The African race seem to enjoy an immunity from fevers in regions where other races suffer severely; so that although the climate of Soopah was occasionally very feverish for Hindoos, the Sidhis never found it unhealthy.

Katijah Beebee, a woman of this race, who had the strength and courage of a man, and for years wore male attire and passed for a man, was the heroine of various local tales. She enlisted as a peon, and served for some years at the talook cutcheri in that capacity; then she became a daring and successful smuggler, and when she was caught at last, she (like Dirk Hatteraick) offered a resistance which it took several strong men to overpower.

This forest land possessed a splendid breed of buffaloes, vastly superior to the bare-skinned, ungainly creatures common in the plains of India. Shaggy-haired, massive, and short jointed, with short, thick, symmetrically curved horns, the Soopah buffaloes possessed immense strength, and could drag very heavy loads.

A bull of this breed is a match for a tiger. On one occasion a herd of buffaloes with their calves was menaced by a tiger while grazing on the skirts of the forest. The tiger tried by roaring to stampede the herd, and the herdsman, shouting and beating the ground with his heavy quarter-staff, was endeavouring to drive him off. Presently the tiger sprang at the man and knocked him down, but as the brute stood over him growling, the bull of the herd charged home, rolled the tiger over and put him to flight; the only injury the man sustained was a wound in the leg from the horn of his friend the bull, inflicted as it knocked over the tiger.

The bison, a much larger animal than the buffalo, is extensively found in North Canara, but I reserve a description of this noblest of its *feræ* for a later chapter.

Soopah is the only region in which I have met with the toucan, or great hornbill, the lesser kinds of hornbill are common in many parts of India. I was walking one morning through the forest in the north-eastern part of Soopah, when a bird of unusual size passed overhead among the tops of the lofty trees. I sent a random bullet after him which neither harmed nor alarmed him, as I presently saw him perch among the topmost boughs of a high tree some distance in advance.

As I walked quietly towards the tree, I saw the comical looking head with its huge aquiline beak, regarding me through a fork in the branch; and I account it one of the best shots I ever made, when I sent a ball from a light, smooth-bore Westley Richards through the head just at its junction with the handsome orange-coloured helmet which surmounts it. Down came the toucan with outspread wings, dead apparently; but when my peon Manoel raised him by the thick muscular neck, he fastened his great claws on his hand, and made the wood resound with a succession of roars more like a bull than a bird. He lived at least an hour, and roared all the way home to the tents.

The head of the toucan, including the helmet and beak, must be nearly fifteen inches long, the rest of the bird being rather longer than this; the legs are short, and only fitted for climbing about the branches, to which the large strong talons are also adapted. The plumage is black and white, the beak and helmet alone being of a beautiful shaded orange. A gland on the back, above the tail, supplies the pigment for this colouring, which is applied by the bird itself, its leisure moments seeming to be all passed in rubbing the beak and helmet on this gland, a process which involves the adoption of a most uncomfortable-looking position.

CHAPTER III.

BELIKERI.

Before leaving the Bálaghaut, or upper country, I visited Hullial, where Captain Coode was in command of a detachment of the 35th Regiment of Native Infantry, watching the Soopah forests. I then went on to Sirci, where the rest of the Regiment was held in reserve, and sending for my wife and child from Mangalore, returned to Belikeri.

Our house at Belikeri, situated as I have already said on a promontory between two bays of great natural beauty, was built on a cliff of red laterite. This curious rock is rather soft and cheese-like when first quarried, but hardens rapidly when exposed to the air; it is full of the same sort of holes as are to be found in *gruyère*, but it makes very good building material, and the walls of our house were built of slabs quarried on the spot. The whole cliff was full of fissures and caves on its sea face, and the various shrubs and trees which grew about the house and grounds seemed to root themselves readily, notwithstanding the unpromising hardness of the surface.

Notable among the surrounding shrubs was the nux vomica, which yields the deadly strychnine; it is in fact rather a tree than a shrub, as it attains a height of from fifteen to twenty feet. The leaves are of a very dark green, hard, shining, and brittle, and resemble those of the cinnamon in having two longitudinal fibres which divide the leaf into three parts. The fruit is of the same dark green colour as the leaves, and is just the size of a tennis ball. When it is ripe the rind breaks easily and discloses a bright orange-coloured pulp in which are flat brown seeds of the size of a shilling. The pulp is eaten freely by birds, and must therefore be harmless, the strychnine is contained in the seeds (which the birds never touch) and in the rind and leaves.

Near at hand were two or three wild

mangosteen trees; the crimson rind of the fruit and its pearly white contents exactly resemble those of the cultivated mangosteen in appearance, but are intensely sour. The same gamboge resin distils from both trees, and furnishes I think the gamboge of commerce.

Towards the end of the promontory the sea at high water and in storms dashed against the cliff, and here was a large cave in which a troop of sea otters generally harboured. The floor of the cliff was under water, but as it was piled with laterite boulders for many feet above sea level, the otters were provided with absolutely impregnable fastnesses under the boulders and in the labyrinth of interstices which they formed. I often watched them in the sea from the cliff above their cave, and used to try my rifle upon them; but as they invariably dived to the flash of the gun, I never got one, and I cannot tell whether the sea otter differs from the kind which frequents the streams inland. I got a fine specimen of the latter kind one morning on the Mysore border, while strolling along a glade between the bamboo jungle and a pretty stream, and looking for peafowl. A whole family of otters rushed headlong down from the jungle to the stream. I rolled over the last of the party, and found I had killed a fine dog otter nearly three feet long. The skin is russet brown, with close-set, glossy fur.

One morning as I was swimming out to a rock in the bay south of the house, a large otter raised himself in the water a few paces in advance of me. With his head and shoulders above the surface, he looked like a mermaid, and testified his astonishment and displeasure by spitting like a cat and uttering a little shrill bark like a puppy. In order to frighten him thoroughly and prevent his diving at my feet, I made at him splashing and shouting; on this he disappeared, and as I climbed my rock for a header, I saw him land and scamper up among the rocks. Probably he was in doubt as to what manner of animal was approaching him, and abandoned hostile ideas when he saw it was a man.

In smaller caves and fissures in our cliff dwelt sundry porcupines, shy, nocturnal creatures whom I did not care to molest, as we had nothing in the garden to tempt them to mischief. I often found their quills, but only on one occasion fell in with the animal accidentally. This was when I was starting for a ride very early in the morning, at a season when the grass was long. A poligar dog that was with me started off in pursuit of what I took to be one of our turkey cocks. Riding up to whip off the dog, I found he was chasing a large porcupine whose quills were all on end and bristling in self-defence. As the dog could not close with it, I rode the porcupine hither and thither till it took refuge in a bush, when I sent for a gun and shot it. The porcupine makes havoc of melons, pine-apples, and all gourds; but he cannot cross a deep ditch with steep sides, and is thus easily excluded. One of the simplest ways of trapping him is to dig a shelving trench with steep sides narrowing gradually to a width in which the porcupine cannot turn; draw back he cannot, because the set of his quills prevents backing, so that if such a trench is baited with pieces of pine-apple towards the narrow end, the porcupine who follows it is hopelessly involved. On certain occasions porcupines fight desperately, tearing each other frightfully with their long incisor teeth.

On the northern side of the promontory a small river runs into the bay, and the fishing village of Belikeri is close to its *embouchure*. The fishermen and their head man, Byroo, were great allies of mine, and brought me any curiosities of the deep they came across. One day it was a small alligator, which had either been born minus a fore leg or had lost it in infancy. This creature was caught in the nets, and the men had as they thought killed it, but as it completely revived I put a bullet through the throat and killed it. As the alligator received its mortal wound, I was astonished to see it eject from its stomach three good-sized stones; the fishermen assured me that for some reason or other alligators are in the habit of swallowing stones.

This power of ejecting what it has swallowed was curiously exemplified a little while later. A pretty little Blenheim spaniel belonging to a visitor was one morning seized and carried off at a spot where the shallow water from a small stream rolled over the sands into the sea.

My friend and I hurried down gun in hand to avenge poor little Nap, the alligator had of course disappeared, and we walked up the course of the stream as it wound among the fields, each of us taking a separate bank. Presently I saw the alligator sailing down the stream towards me, with his head held a little above water; I instantly gave him both barrels at the junction of the head and throat. The brute threw his whole length clean out of the water and then disappeared. We searched the bottom all over for his carcass without success, but found the body of the little dog. This was quite four hundred yards from the spot where he had been seized, and it was clear that the alligator on being hit had ejected the dog. There was neither tooth mark nor wound of any kind visible on the body.

I used often to see alligators asleep on the sandy beach with their mouths wide open, and found that, as in the case of the shark, the act of opening the jaws draws a tough white membrane across the gullet, effectually closing it and preventing the water from rushing in so long as the jaws remain open.

In the month of October, when the south-west monsoon has spent its force and before the wind from the north-east begins to blow, there are a few weeks of profound calm on the waters of the western coast. At this season large fish of various kinds rise to the surface and lie there basking in the sun; our bay used to be covered with canoes every day and all day during this period, and the fishermen were busy killing the fish with the harpoon.

I once joined them and tried my hand at the harpoon, but without much success. The fish lay a little below the surface, and practice was required in order to throw with accuracy. The arrangement of the harpoon is very ingenious: the head fits loosely to the shaft, and disengages itself when a fish is struck; a separate rope connects it with the boat, and as merely a few feet of cord attaches the shaft to the disengaged head, it serves as a float to indicate the course of the wounded fish.

One afternoon in November, Byroo and some thirty or forty fishermen with him came up to the house dragging a great saw-fish, which measured about twenty-one feet from the end of the saw to the tail, and was quite two feet thick at the head, from which point it tapered down to the tail. The breadth across the belly under the shoulders was between two and three feet. I found on examining the fish that the saw or double rake was set in the same plane as the belly, which was perfectly flat; and the mouth, which was a mere slit of about eight inches wide, was not far behind the root of the saw. The fish could not possibly open such a mouth to any width, but moving flat along the bottom, and swaying the rake from side to side as it advanced, it would detach weed and shell-fish and sea-slugs from the bed of the sea, and these might be sucked into the mouth as it passed over them.

I am not, I regret to say, a scientific naturalist, and I offer this theory of the saw-fish and his manner of gaining his living for what it may be worth.

On that occasion I stupidly missed a golden opportunity for verifying my theory.* I had satisfied my curiosity,

* By neglecting to open the fish.

and was about to dismiss Byroo with a present, when he asked for further orders. "It once happened, sahib, that a very large fish was taken, and in its belly was found a box of treasure; ever since then there has been a Circar order that no large fish shall be cut up without the sanction of a Government officer."

The capture of this monster had taxed the utmost energies of three or four boats' crews and occupied them fully four hours. I preserved the rake (or saw as it is inappropriately called) of this fish for many years; it was about three feet long. I have lost it, but have hanging up in my hall a still larger specimen of the same weapon. It merits this name (though its primary use must be what I have suggested) because a side blow with the row of sharp, horny teeth would inflict a fearful wound on an assailant.

I had often picked up on the beach after a storm the shells of the pearl oyster: beautiful mother-of-pearl, not of the thick, massive kind found in the Persian gulf, but identical I believe with the pearl oysters of Ceylon.

Wishing to examine the bed from which these shells came, I one day took Byroo and four or five skilful divers in my sailing boat to the head of the bay, to test the contents of the shells. We collected about five hundred shells, which were at once opened and searched; but beyond a number of tiny seed-pearls and one irregularly shaped pearl, about as large as a sweet pea, I found nothing of value. My specimens were duly forwarded to Madras, but the Government were not disposed to open a fishery.

One day when I was out in camp holding office in a tent, a large iguana, whose hole may have been accidentally enclosed by the tent walls, suddenly found itself, to its great alarm, in the midst of the conclave of writers in white calico, bundles of papers, rugs, and ink-stands. The lizard was between two and three feet long, and as it rushed blindly round and round, seeking a way of escape, it created quite as much horror and confusion among my Brahmin scribes as it felt, careering over them and their carpets till it at last found an exit.

When tranquillity was restored, one

of my moonshis, José Prebhoo, a Concani of one of the numerous families descended from Xavier's converts, gravely informed me that in the old days iguanas were used in gaining access to besieged places; for, said he, "A large iguana, sahib, is so strong that if three or four men laid hold of its tail he could drag them up a wall or a tree"! This José Prebhoo was full of stories, and constituted himself *raconteur* general of the establishment, never losing an opportunity to edge in a story if possible. News came one day that the post runner had been delayed some hours between Belikeri and Sedasheghur by a tigress which lay down across the path at a spot where it crossed a spur of the hills. The runner tried all he knew to frighten the tigress away, shouting, banging his bell stick on the ground, and abusing her vilely; the brute merely roared back at him, and would not move till he collected a sufficient number of allies to overawe her. This news immediately inspired our *raconteur* to cite a parallel incident.

"Once upon a time, sahib, there was a postal runner who was a very brave and strong man. A bear met him between Yellapore and Hullial, and tried to seize him; but the runner slipped behind a tree so cleverly that the bear seized the tree. Upon this the runner laid hold of the bear's fore legs, set his own feet against the tree, and being very strong he ground the bear against it; and the more he pulled, the tighter the bear hugged the tree, until at last the bear was killed, and the runner got the Government reward."

During one rainy season, when the weather at Belikeri had been unusually stormy, I happened to enter, in search of something, the bath-room attached to a room not then in use. It was getting dark, and I had a candle with me; just as I was leaving the bath-room, a pile of stones in one corner of the bathing place caught my eye, and I turned to look at it. As I held the candle towards it, the seeming pile of stones resolved itself into the spotted coils of a python, which lay there, coil over coil, with its head resting on the topmost coil, and the bright eyes watching my movements.

Evidently the snake had entered through a hole of four or five inches square by which the water escaped, and he might at any moment retreat by the same way; so I shouted for a gun and a big stick, and presently Kistnama, one of my Lascars, rushed in with a gun and two stout staves. One barrel was loaded, and I instantly fired at the head; but either the snake moved or the light deceived me, and he reared himself up at us higher than our heads. Then we belaboured him with all our strength, and in a second or two beat him down, so that he fell across the low wall which enclosed the bathing-place; in that position our blows broke the snake's spine, so that he could not raise himself again, and we soon finished him. Dragged outside and measured, this snake proved to be about eleven feet long, and twelve inches in girth round the belly at the thickest part.

Probably our poultry yard was the attraction which led the python to take up his quarters with us, and the quiet and shelter of the bath-room afforded a convenient refuge from the rain.

I witnessed another combat one morning on the beach, between antagonists of very different calibre. A large black sand wasp was busy excavating a gallery in the compact moist sand just above high-water mark, kicking out with his long hind legs the pellets of sand he dug out. Presently a silvery little crab, no bigger than a threepenny bit, darted out of an adjoining hole and made at the wasp with great fury, trying to seize it with his great fighting claw. The wasp troubled himself very little; he simply rose an inch or two from the sand and swooped at the crab from behind, avoiding the brandished claw, and obliging the crab to *pirouette* round and round in an absurd and fatiguing manner, so that he was soon obliged to retreat to his hole for a rest. But he was out again in an instant, and renewed the battle as eagerly but with no better success than before. I do not think he appeared for a third round, and I regretted not being able to advise him to countermine the wasp and engage him underground when he resumed his excavation, which he presently did with great *sang froid*.

I have never seen mention of what I one day observed, to wit, that the blue-bottle fly eats ant's eggs. A long train of tiny ants, each carrying a white egg, was crossing the veranda; a blue-bottle fly alighted close by, and from time to time rose and hovered close above the caravan; the wind from his wings blew the ants about, and some of them dropped their loads, these were instantly raised one by one by the fly at the end of his proboscis, sucked, and then dropped; and whenever a fresh supply was wanted, the fly rose on his wings and winnowed the line of ants. No attempt was made by any of them to turn upon the fly or molest it.

CHAPTER IV.

HONAMA AND HIS MEN.

ABOUT two miles from Belikeri Bay was a village inhabited by Canarese ryots, who cultivated rice in the low-lying fields round their houses, and dry grain crops of various kinds in forest clearings, and who largely supplemented their food supply by netting and spearing hog, deer, and elk in the jungles. Unlike Byroo and his fishermen, who were Roman Catholics, descendants of Xavier's converts, Honama and his brethren were Hindoos, and of a different race from the fishing population on the coast.

The system of forest cultivation was rude but very successful. A hill side was chosen covered with the less valuable and smaller kinds of trees, these were felled and burnt during the hot dry months of March, April, and May; then the ashes were roughly levelled and sown with millet or pulse, and the space was protected by a strong, rude fence. During the rains a luxuriant crop sprung up, and an almost equally good one could be raised in the second year. Then the plot was abandoned, and left untouched for ten or twelve years, by the end of which period the copious rainfall and the tropical sun had reclothed it with a forest growth of sufficient dimensions for a repetition of the felling and burning. This kind of cultivation was called "coomeri," and though seemingly wasteful, suited the conditions under which a sparse population contended with the ever encroaching forest.

Such a life necessarily familiarized the Canarese ryot with every glade and hill and valley within many miles of his home, and acquainted him with the habits of the wild creatures which harboured there, making him by habit, as well as taste, a practised shikari. Honama and his men always accompanied me on my beats for bison, elk, or deer, and I sometimes joined them when they took out their nets to hunt on their own account. On these occasions they speared any creature that came into the net, leopards, hyenas, and even tigers, as well as deer or hog, but they never attempted to deal with bison in this way. When I was with them, my friends made it a point of etiquette that I should give the *coup de grace* to any animal of mark, and I once had to come from my post beyond the net, and put an end to a leopard which was pinned helpless to the ground, on its back, by two spears through the loose skin of the neck.

The nets were made of the tough rope twisted by the hunters themselves, from the fibre of the pandanus, or wild pine-apple, which abounds all over southern India. When these nets were reared for game, a long lane of about twelve feet wide was cleared, intersecting the runs followed by wild animals in passing from any given stretch of outlying jungle to the deeper forest. The bottom of the net was firmly pegged down along its whole length; the upper side was then raised by props (like the clothes lines in a drying ground) to a height of about ten feet, the main support being given to the net by props on the side from which animals would approach it when roused by the beaters; by every one of these latter props crouched a spearman under an extemporised screen of brushwood, and with his goat's-hair blanket folded on his shoulders. The instant that an animal rushed against the net, the spearmen knocked away the props next to them, and the net yielding to the pressure of the props on the further side, fell inwards upon the struggling beast, which was at once speared.

On one occasion we took out the nets with the intention of netting a tiger that had killed several cows in the neighbourhood ; but though we spent the whole day till four in the afternoon, in beating all the most likely coverts, we saw nothing of the tiger, and only brought home a spotted deer. I left Honama and the rest on their way home, and rode back to Belikeri. I had scarcely bathed and eaten, when a breathless shikari rushed up to the house to say the tiger was found in a patch of scrub jungle close to Honama's village, where he had killed and partly eaten one of their cows while we were beating for him at a distance.

I rode off directly, but before I reached the spot met a triumphant procession carrying the dead tiger. I then learned that the nets had been at once pitched and a beat commenced, but that the tiger had shown himself in so savage a mood that both the beaters and the spearmen, whose post was inside the net, had been cowed, and that the latter had left their usual posts and got behind the net. The tiger, however, of his own accord made at the net, and rearing himself up, placed his two fore paws against it; there was no one to knock away the inner props at this critical moment, the tiger was roaring angrily, and struggling to force back the net, which might at any moment fall in the wrong direction.

Then old Honama pulled himself together, and taking his spear in both hands, struck it into the tiger's open mouth, with the result of making him topple backwards, dragging the net down upon him. The spearmen were upon him in an instant, pinning him down and gashing him mercilessly, a peon of mine who lived in that same village, fired an old musket into him, and all was over. This was an enormous tiger, and the size and weight of his fore arm and paw were terrible to see.

The town and fort of Ancola were about three miles south of Belikeri. An open bay, with a broad, level shore of firm sand, extended from our promontory to the rocky headland which closed its southern end, and the approach to the town was by this sandy beach. The fort was a massive rectangular enclosure, a relic of the old days of Mahratta supremacy, standing between the hills and the town in a position either to protect or overawe its inhabitants. Nothing remained of the buildings inside the enclosure but roofless and ruinous walls, and a few vaults under ground. Ancola itself was a little old-world looking town, embowered in groves of mango, jack, and cocoa-nut trees; the bazaar in its main street was screened from the sun by scaffolding and canopy, as at Cairo, and on the tiled roofs of its ancient houses the grass grew tall and thick enough for the mower. No great thoroughfare passed through the quiet streets, and an air of sleepy cheerfulness pervaded the whole place.

Some years before I reached Canara, the town of Ancola had passed through a brief reign of terror and grief. A man-eater had taken up its abode in the neighbourhood, and for some time, at intervals of a few days, one victim after another, generally a woman or a child, was carried off. Sometimes a sleeping person, in a position of fancied security, was seized and dragged away, and for a time all attempts to intercept and kill the murderer were baffled by its cunning and boldness. The little community was beside itself with grief and horror. At last it was discovered that the man-eater had its lair not in the forest, but in a vault of the ruined fort, and the whole male population armed, and mobbed it in its den, killing not a tiger, as was supposed, but a leopard.[1]

News was one day brought to me that a leopard had again been seen near Ancola, and had killed cattle; and as there was a natural anxiety to be rid of it, I lost no time in summoning Honama and his men to join me, with their nets, and exterminate the enemy. A long wooded spur of the hills ends at Ancola, and gives access by the Arbyle Ghaut to the tableland of Soopah. The leopard was tracked into the heavy jungle at the end of this

[1] "A leopard shall watch over their cities."

spur, a mile or two from Ancola, and the nets were pitched so as to intercept the brute on his way upward. I took post on the right flank of the net, and a little in advance of it, and ensconced myself and my little henchman, Manoel, who always carried my second gun, among the leafy boughs of a small sapling.

The beaters had the greatest difficulty in forcing this leopard from his haunts. We heard him roar repeatedly in one part of the jungle or another; twice the spearmen saw him come close to the nets and then double back, and had not the numerous *posse* of beaters, aided by the din and discord of many drums, horns, and cymbals, stuck bravely to their work for at least two hours, the leopard would have made his way back. He was driven a third time towards the nets, near my post, and was again doubling back when I caught sight of an orange-coloured mass gliding through the underwood. Just in front of him was a little open space which he must cross, and there I dropped him dead with a bullet aimed high up behind the shoulder, just below the spine.

A considerable experience in shooting large game has convinced me that this is *par excellence* the vital point, and that a wound here is more instantaneously fatal than one low down behind the shoulder. Three times elk, which I have wounded low down behind the shoulder, have run from fifty to a hundred yards before dropping. This leopard neither stirred nor spoke after he was hit, except that as the body was being carried down the hill, half an hour later, slung under a pole, the jaws distended convulsively, and a deep sound, half gurgle, half growl, issued from the chest. The startled carriers nearly dropped their load, but were soon reassured that the creature was really dead.

I had found it difficult to prevent the spearmen from spoiling the skin by plunging their spears into the dead leopard, and to show them there was no life left in him, I laid hold of the tail and shook it. "O sahib! don't do that!" they cried; "if you shake their tails they always revive!"

As I walked down the ghaut that morning, towards Ancola, I noticed something stirring in a puddle left by the rain of the previous day, and, stopping to look, found a tiny fish, about an inch long, and shaped like a roach or carp. Neither pond nor stream was near; the puddle was rain-water, and the fish was well and lively; how came it there? I can only conclude that it came down—as fish have been known to do—in the shower, and that if others fell at the same time on the path, birds or beasts must have carried them off.

Another leopard was killed during the rains, near Sedasheghur, seventeen miles north of Belikeri, in a very gallant manner by a fine young fellow of the same race as my friends the spearmen. Wild animals find the deeper forests unpleasant quarters in the monsoon rains; cloudy skies, frequent showers, the perpetual drip from the trees, and above all the persecution of the tiny jungle leeches, drive them to the more open glades, where they have the benefit of occasional sunshine; and at such seasons they are at no great distance from human habitations. Thus it happened that the leopard in question was found at daylight in the middle of a small hamlet, trying to conceal itself under the low, projecting eaves of one of the huts.

There were no fire-arms at hand, so the young fellow who discovered the leopard, folding his goat's-hair blanket over his left arm, and armed with his sharp sickle-shaped wood-knife, made at the brute, and receiving its spring on his left arm and shoulder, gashed it so terribly about the vitals that he killed it without sustaining any very serious injuries to himself. His shoulder was a little torn by the leopard's claws, and he was slightly bitten on the arm where the leopard had got its teeth through the folds of the blanket; but that was all.

The skin was brought in to me for the usual reward, and I saw that the leopard was of no great size, but still a very formidable antagonist. Its conqueror was a remarkably handsome young man, and looked like a bronze cast of the Apollo.

Not far from the scene of this exploit I once beat the neighbouring woods for three successive days for a tiger which was reported to have killed a man. Two companions from Sedasheghur were with me, and all the local shikaries; but unfortunately we had no nets, and my friend Honama, and his spearmen, though invaluable allies in their own jungles, where every glade was familiar ground, always confined themselves to their own neighbourhood.

The result was that the tiger, though several times seen by the beaters, never gave us a shot, out-manœuvring us cleverly on every occasion. On the third day, as we walked along a path between two woods, to take up a fresh position, one of my companions being about fifty yards in advance, and the other as far behind me, I heard the latter call to me; but as he did not signal by whistling, to signify that anything was in sight, I did not stop on the instant. Presently he came up breathless, "O Mr. Forbes, the tiger has just crossed the path not three paces behind you." He had given his gun to a follower to carry, but I had mine on my shoulder, and had I turned when he spoke, I might have been tempted to fire, which is a very dangerous proceeding when face to face with a tiger. Even with this evidence of the tiger's whereabouts, we did not succeed in getting a shot at him; but as he was not again seen or heard of after that day, he probably left the neighbourhood in disgust.

It has been thought that the safest position in tiger-shooting is in a tree; but a fatal incident in the Hyderabad country has shown that unless the sportsman is at a considerable height from the ground he is liable to be seized.

Four officers, with one of whom I was well acquainted, went out to beat for a tigress in the neighbourhood of Hyderabad. They posted themselves in the usual way at intervals on the outskirts of the jungle; one at least of the number being on the branch of a tree with a shikari beside him. During the beat the tigress showed great irritation, and knocked over one of the beaters. She reached the edge of the jungle opposite the tree in question, and instead of moving stealthily out, she charged instantly for the tree, and reaching the branch in a single bound, tore down the shikari. The officer at once fired and wounded her; on which she again sprung into the tree, pulled him down also, and began worrying him. The poor fellow was remarkably strong and athletic, and fought desperately for his life. His three companions hearing the outcry hurried up, and putting shoulder to shoulder walked up to the tigress and killed her on the spot. But both their friend and the shikari died from the injuries they had sustained, while they were being carried in to Hyderabad.

CHAPTER V.

GOKERN AND YÁANA. THE BISON.

GOKERN is the name of a very ancient temple of great repute for sanctity among the Hindoos of western India. The temple and the little town which has grown up round it are built on the shore of a pretty sheltered cove lined with cocoa-nut palms. Close behind the temple rise two steep conical hills covered with short turf; these hills are united at their base, round which the houses nestle closely. They are precisely equal in height and of similar shape, and when looked at from the sea, exactly embody

ANCOLA & GOKERN HEADLANDS.

the idea conveyed in the name Gokern, which means cow's ears. Seen from above, against the intense blue of the sea, the miniature town, with its quaintly fashioned red stone temple half hidden by foliage, is a gem for a painter. Gokern was generally a very tranquil little place, but at certain festivals numerous pilgrims assembled there, some of whom came from a distance. Those from the north passed through Belikeri, and one evening an unfortunate pilgrim was brought to me in a litter, who had come to cruel grief on his way. He was found disabled in a forest clearing, and stated that having wandered out of the way between Sedasheghur and Belikeri, he had met four bears in the jungle, (probably two full-grown bears and their cubs); three of the four ran away, but the fourth attacked him and mangled him terribly. When the bear left him, he had managed to climb into a raised stage in the clearing, used by watchers at crop time, and there he was found. When brought to me, the poor fellow was delirious; the bear had scalped him, and injured the skull so as to expose the brain, while the skin of the forehead and nose were torn downward and overhung the mouth, giving the face a strange animal appearance. In spite of these injuries he did not seem to be in pain, but sat up and talked wildly, fancying himself a raja, and inviting me to sit beside him. He was carried in at once to the small military hospital at Sedasheghur, but did not long survive.

It is a strange thing that the bear should always endeavour to tear the head and face when it attacks a man; the native idea is that it seeks to get at the brain and devour it, and I conclude that this is really the case, as the head is invariably the object of attack.

I once introduced a tame, half-grown bear to a large turtle; without a moment's hesitation the bear planted all four feet on the turtle and began to try and tear off the upper shell in a business-like way, which would no doubt have been successful if we had not interfered. As this bear had been with us from its infancy, and had never seen a turtle, its proceedings must have been the result of a very strong instinct indeed.

From Gokern the bands of pilgrims

generally made their way to the rocks of Yáana, a strange, weird spot, remote from human abodes, and just on the eastern border of the Ancola forest, where the trees give place to grassy, open downs. A Hindoo sunygási, or hermit, lived in a cave under the overhanging rock, and received the offerings of pilgrims.

On the upper part of the rock, and in a position inaccessible both from above and below, hung in numbers the combs and nests of wild bees. In the old times it is said that on certain occasions all the women of Gokern and the surrounding country marched in procession round these rocks. The bees watched the devotees as they passed, and if there chanced to be among them any woman whose conduct was not blameless, down came the bees upon her in wrath and punished her frailty.

It is not surprising that this custom had died out long since; and whatever may be the moral sensitiveness of bees, it is quite certain that any procession passing round the rock below their nests would be sure to bring down these vindictive little savages. Doctor Schweinfurth's account of the attack on him and his crew on his way up the Nile is an instance of the danger of provoking them; and an officer of my acquaintance who was engaged on a boundary survey in central India, suffered most severely. He and his surveyors unluckily roused a swarm of wild bees on a rocky hill. Away went the whole surveying party in headlong stampede; but my friend as he ran had the misfortune to trip and fall, and was instantly covered. A friendly shepherd partly beat off the bees, and covered the victim with his blanket; but for the next twenty-four hours Captain D—'s servants were busy extracting the multitude of stings left sticking in him.

I was assured by the Tahsildar of Ancola that the rocks of Yáana had only once, a long time ago, been visited by a European, and he often begged me to go and see the spot; so I at last sent out a small tent, and rode out.

After crossing the forest the path for some miles led along its borders, and as I rode from one green hill to another, I began to catch glimpses at intervals of clusters of sharp spires and dark pinnacles rising above the trees. I seemed to be approaching some lofty abbey in the wilderness, of vast and irregular dimensions. At last I came suddenly on a wide *enceinte*, bare alike of tree and herb, black, and strewn with ashes, as if some recent conflagration had consumed the very ground as well as what grew upon it. In the centre of this charred and desolate space rose the black rocks of Yáana, a pile of perhaps two hundred feet high, and about three times as much in circumference. In shape the mass seemed like a vast tussock with countless pointed tops, solid indeed for half its height, but split and shivered in its upper half. One deep rift alone reached to the very base, and sundered the rock into two parts.

Here, says the Hindoo legend, a rákshasa flying from a more powerful demon than himself, broke through the solid rock and was followed by his pursuer. Beyond suchlike childish myths, local tradition has no explanation to offer of the marvel. Hindoo history records no volcanic disturbance, no natural convulsion of overwhelming violence. As the shattered rocks and the blackened earth are now, so they have been from a time beyond the ken of man; a strange, portentous sight, evidencing the action of forces of volcanic violence, though not displayed in the usual manner.

When a tract of forest is felled and burnt, a single monsoon covers the ashes with vegetation, but at Yáana centuries have not won a blade of grass from the dead ground. Nearly forty years have passed since I stood and wondered beneath those rocks, and I think it is certain that since that time they have been visited and described by observers more competent than myself to divine the nature of the catastrophe which has left them to a desolation like that of the Dead Sea.

In describing the manner in which Honama and his fellows set up their nets for wild animals, I mentioned that these hardy hunters never attempted to drive the bison towards them. These grand-looking creatures would sweep the nets before them by sheer momentum.

Persons who have not made acquaintance with the bison of south-western India might not unreasonably suppose the animal to be a variety of the wild buffalo or auroch of America; but there is in fact no resemblance whatever between the two. The Indian bison is as large again as the wild buffalo; it has a different number of ribs, and a head differently set on; it has no mane, and is beside distinguished by a peculiarity to be found in no other member of the bovine race. This consists of a bony horizontal ridge or wither, which extends from the neck half-way along the back, where it ends abruptly; it adds five or six inches at least to the height of the animal's forehand, and gives it immense strength and mass. When the bison crashes through the thickets in his irresistible hand-gallop the horns are thrown back, so as not to catch the boughs, and the shock of contact falls on the solid base of the horns, and on the dorsal ridge aforesaid. This elongated and exaggerated wither gives the animal an outline unlike that of any other creature; nevertheless the bison is a very noble-looking beast. The colour is a dark bluish slate, shaded with red, and the lower parts of the legs are of a light tawny hue. The horns, starting from very massive bases, describe a wide and symmetrical curve. From the time the animal is five years old every season contributes a spiral ring at the base of the horn, and as bisons have been shot whose horns showed nine and even ten of these rings, it follows that they attain at least the age of fifteen years.

The dorsal ridge in full-grown bulls makes the measurement both of height and girth reach rather startling figures. I have myself assisted at the death of a bull bison which, as he lay dead, measured nineteen hands from the point of the hoof to the top of the wither; his girth behind the shoulder and over the wither was nine feet some inches. This bull was shot at Gairsappa, on the ridge overhanging the precipitous ravine (a thousand feet deep) into which the river plunges. My companion who was on the ridge crippled the bison by a bullet in the shoulder, and I ascended the bare hill-side from a valley below to cut off his retreat; when within twenty paces or so, I raised the rifle for a shot, but the cap had fallen off as I ran, and I should have fared badly but for the bull's wounded shoulder. He lowered his head to charge down on me, but rolled over and fell as often as he attempted to repeat the charge. I am sorry to say that the poor bull received a good many bullets before he was killed, though we were both most anxious to end his sufferings.

I was more fortunate with the first bull I ever shot, and succeeded—by aiming high up behind the shoulder, and a few inches under the base of the dorsal ridge—in dropping him with a single ball from a smooth bore; he measured seventeen hands two inches, and his head and horns are still preserved in a friend's collection in Scotland.

Word was brought me one morning that a small herd of bison were lying down in an open glade in the Ancola forest, not far from Belikeri. I started for a stalk with the shikari who brought the news, and Manoel, a little Concani peon who always carried my second gun. The herd had risen before we reached the spot, leaving the impress of their bulky forms on the long grass, and we tracked them to a steep stony hill, densely covered with a growth of bastard bamboo cane.

As we ascended cautiously, it was easy to follow in the bison's wake, marked as it was by bent and trampled cane, and we now and then picked up fragments of the tender green shoots which had dropped from their mouths as they browsed upwards; but on either side the trail it was impossible to see a yard, so dense was the canebrake. Still we followed, creeping on more and more carefully. At last we stopped in uncertainty: a strong atmosphere as of a cow-house surrounded us, and we became conscious that we were in the midst of the herd. We listened and peered round intently, but could neither see anything nor hear a sound. Then on a sudden there was a rush like thunder, and we all crouched low, expecting to be trampled down. The thicket crashed and swayed, and the stones clattered down as the avalanche of bison swept by us and round us;

but beyond a dim twinkling of tawny legs among the canes, I could make out no distinct form, and of course did not attempt to fire. The wild herd were aware of us, and instinctively avoided us in their rush; but they could not have seen more of us than we did of them.

I once killed a bull bison near Nágwádi, on the Mysore border, and learned why it is that the head of the animal seems so nearly invulnerable. It was in the sultry month of May, and the grass had been burnt on the bare hills outside the forests. A herd of bison broke cover and crossed a bare and blackened plain on their way to the opposite jungle. A handsome bull, just full grown, led the herd, and as they passed in front of my ambush, about a hundred yards off, I fired a shot at the bull from a single barrelled rifle, aiming well in front of him, in the hope of striking the shoulder. I had aimed too far forward, the bullet passed through the dewlap; but as the wound bled sufficiently for an able tracker to follow the trail, Manoel and the shikari and I entered the jungle in pursuit. After we had toiled for some distance under a scorching sun, the tracker stopped, and explaining that the bull was bound for a particular moist and shady spot in the deeper forest, he promised by making a rapid *detour* to anticipate its arrival there and bring me face to face with it. Sure enough, we were first at the spot, but Manoel and I had not been ensconced five minutes in a leafy thicket when we heard the bull approaching leisurely. Immediately in front of us was a beautiful green glade of about seventy yards wide, and on the opposite edge of this space the bull presently emerged, he was exactly facing us, and stopping as he reached the open, remained for some minutes motionless.

At last I began to fear he would suddenly turn and retreat; a side shot he would not give, but I could see his eye as his head turned slightly sideways, and setting the hair trigger of the rifle, I aimed with extreme care in the hopes of reaching the brain through the eye. The bull seemed confused by the shot, but presently galloped straight at our thicket. I glanced round for a tree, but none was near enough. Manoel thrust the Westley Richards into my hand, and drawing back a pace or two as the bull crashed through the bushes, I fired both barrels into him behind the shoulder. He stopped almost at once, and staggered to and fro in the vain effort to keep his feet, and came heavily to the ground, Manoel calmly walking up to him as he tottered, and superintending his last moments. We at once looked to see where the rifle ball had struck, and found it had entered just above the right eye, and passing obliquely through the solid bone of the forehead, had gone out at the base of the opposite horn; further examination showed that the horns were bedded in a plate of cellular bone which covers no portion of the brain anywhere above the eyes. This bull was not more than five years old, and I have no doubt that in an older animal the cellular plate of bone would become quite solid. This arrangement renders it a matter of indifference to the bison how much he is hit about the upper part of the head, his most vulnerable points are behind the shoulder and just behind the angle of the jaw, where the throat begins.

It is due to one of the bravest and ugliest little men that ever stepped, that I should describe my henchman Manoel. A short, square, wiry figure supported a very large head; the face was broad, the mouth wide, the eyes goggle, and the ears were large and projecting. But this unpromising tabernacle was the abode of a gallant spirit, and I could count upon Manoel in any moment of danger. I had often trouble in restraining him from taking dangerous liberties with wounded animals. No doubt a life in or near great forests, where wild animals abound, leads to a certain familiarity with their nature and habits which enables men so situated to know exactly how far they may count on the fear or indifference of wild beasts; but to lay hold of a wounded bison by the horn is scarcely to be justified on those grounds.

An example of a different kind will show, however, that there was nothing of bravado about Manoel. We were one day fording a rapid stream in the jungles, nearly four feet deep, when Manoel, who was behind me carrying my gun, was suddenly taken off his legs and disappeared completely under water for a second or two, all except the hand which held my gun; the hand and gun alone were visible above the surface, and when a comrade dragged him up, the gun was still untouched by the water.

CHAPTER VI.

SIRCI. NEELCOOND. GAIRSAPPA.

SIRCI is a considerable town, twenty miles south of Soopah, and situated in a wide plain everywhere encircled by the forest. The teak-tree here disappears almost entirely, and gives place to less valuable timber, though the forest is still as dense as ever.

The place was then the head-quarters of the joint magistrate of Canara. My friend, Mr. Samuel Neville Ward, who held the office and was an excellent public servant, was above all things a devoted naturalist, a very mine of interesting lore in regard to the ways of bird and beast, fish and reptile; he was also a draughtsman of rare skill, depicting things too perishable for preservation, and stereotyping in this way peculiarities of attitude and colouring not easy of record by other means. In him the sportsman was effaced in favour of the friendly observer of Nature, who sought the haunts of her wild races not for destruction but for acquaintanceship.

It was his wont to pass many an hour, watching from his concealment, the ways of wild animals. He told me that on one occasion he had seen a string of eight or ten bison walk up in succession to a heavy five-foot fence, and leap lightly over it into the forest clearing it was intended to protect. The proportions of the bison are so massive and so little suggestive of leaping, that I could scarcely have credited them with such a feat on other authority than his. I need scarcely add that my friend never used his gun on these occasions. As regards the protection of crops on forest clearings, the cultivator does not trust wholly to his fences, but watches, sling in hand, on a strong stage, well raised and screened from the rain.

I think Mr. Ward has presented to the British Museum his collection of coloured drawings of over four hundred species of caterpillars. Each is depicted on the leaves it fed upon, and with the chrysalis, shown beside it, into which it shrank; the moth or butterfly, which emerged in due course, was preserved in the usual way, and appended so as to complete the group.

Specimens of all sorts naturally flowed in on a man of such tastes. I remember seeing in his farm-yard during my last visit a fine, vigorous young bison calf, which promised to take kindly to captivity, and raced about the yard after his meals just as happily as any ordinary calf would do. It was a great disappointment when the little bison, suddenly and without visible cause, sickened and died; but not before its owner, true to his instincts, had drawn a faithful likeness of it. I doubt if there is a living specimen in any European collection of the bison of Western India.

About the same time a flying-squirrel, full grown and in perfect health, was brought in; probably it had been taken when young from the nest by its captor, for it seemed perfectly happy in the iron-barred cage into which we put it, a cage which had been prepared for a long-promised but as yet unsecured specimen of the real tiger-cat of that region. Both the flying-squirrel and the tiger-cat are animals of extreme rarity, and I have never before or since seen either of them, either wild or in captivity. The flying-squirrel is the largest of his family, exceeding in size the ordinary brown and orange squirrel of the western forests, which in its turn is four times as large as the squirrel of this country, being in fact about as large as a wild rabbit. The colour of the flying-squirrel is black, shading to iron grey; its length, including the tail, cannot be less than two and a quarter feet, and when the legs are extended in leaping and the membrane which then discloses itself is spread between the hind and fore legs, the whole width of surface is over a foot, and the creature skims through the air like a slate thrown horizontally.

The squirrel had not been in possession of the cage above a day or two when a splendid tiger-cat, orange and black was brought in; there had not been time to prepare a second cage, and so after some hesitation a partition was run across the cage in its centre, dividing it into two compartments, each measuring about eighteen inches by sixteen, and in this way both the strangers seemed to be fairly well lodged and without risk of collision. During the daytime the tiger-cat was quiet, but he made night hideous at intervals by his yells. This went on for two days, but on the morning of the third day the tiger-cat was found growling over the dead body of the poor squirrel, which by some means hard to conjecture he had dragged into his own den, either through the front bars or under the partition. The squirrel was quite dead, but it had not been torn or mangled, and I had the beautiful skin preserved and stuffed, but lost it somehow when I left Canara. The subsequent career of its wanton murderer I do not remember.*

The approaches to Sirci were very impressive. Broad level tracks, cut straight through many a mile of forest, gave access to the seaports of the western coast of India from the inland provinces of Bellary, Belgaum, Darwar, and Mysore, and the cotton, wheat, and other produce raised there was carried on pack cattle, a good deal of it passing through Sirci on its way to the coast.

Here come the hereditary carriers

* Mr. Ward tells me the tiger-cat was sent to England, but died at the mouth of the Thames for want of fresh meat.

ENCAMPMENT AT NEELCOOND.

of southern India, with their countless droves of oxen; clouds of white dust, and the sound of many bells, and the shouts of drovers announce their approach. It is evening, and they are nearing their camping ground, which is not far from the green sward on which my tents are pitched, on the brow of the ghaut at Neelcoond. The stateliest oxen of the drove come first, moving slowly between vast bales of cotton; black tassels hang at the base of their horns, and necklaces of bright brass knobs suspend white shells from their necks. Beasts of less mark follow, and beside them at intervals come stalwart gipsy-looking drovers, staff in hand, attended by large, powerful dogs, not unlike Scotch collies of the larger breed.

Scarcely less imposing in appearance are the women, each with her staff, and sometimes a child carried upon the hip. They wear a petticoat tied at the waist, a spencer above it, and on the head a coloured shawl which falls over the shoulders. Many bangles of brass or glass adorn both the arms and the ankles; the effect of the costume, which differs entirely from that of the Hindoo women, is decidedly picturesque.

These people are Lumbádies, members of the widely spread tribe which has for centuries threaded the forests and bye-ways of India, often provisioning armies in the field (our own among the rest), and always fulfilling their obligations faithfully. In times of peace their office has been to carry to the seaports and salt-works of the Indian coasts the surplus produce of the inland provinces, returning with salt for the supply of their inhabitants. Hardy, persevering, bold, owing nothing to favour, unrivalled in their knowledge of their country, these Lumbádies, or Brinjaries, as they are called in some parts, have rendered services not only valuable, but indispensable to the Indian populations and their rulers. Soon the railroads will have usurped their functions, fulfilling them, of course, far more effectively; but not the less does the "old order" and its service deserve grateful and lasting remembrance.

By this time the bales of cotton are being piled rampart-wise upon the ground, and the camp fires are alight. The sun is just sinking into the western sea, within view of my tents, and all the hill tops are aflame with the sunset colours; but in the deeper and more distant valleys hangs a rich sapphire dimness, like the bloom upon grapes. The chill of sundown is spreading through the forest, and already white mist comes wreathing up from the ravine hard by; it is time to close the tents.

To-morrow morning the Lumbádies and their charge will descend the Dávamunile Ghaut to Meerján. There, on the banks of the broad estuary of the Tuddri, near Gokern, the bales of cotton will be transferred to the ferry boats, and a thousand oxen will take the water and swim across in order to be reloaded for Coompta, seven or eight miles farther on.

As a regiment going into action must count upon some loss, so surely will one and another of the tired cattle give up in mid-stream and turn over on its side, the poor head will droop below the surface, and the distended carcase will float down to the sea. All this because the Parsee merchants from Bombay, having set up their cotton screws and built their warehouses at Coompta, which is an open roadstead, refused to move to Tuddri, where sites were offered them on the shore of a well-protected anchorage. The break of bulk at the ferry, with its wear and tear, the additional stage of carriage to Coompta, the yearly loss of cattle to the Lumbádies, the risks of the open roadstead to the country craft,—all these counted for nothing in comparison with the cost and trouble of moving a few miles up the coast.

In 1848 an experienced engineer officer, General Frederick Cotton, visited the Tuddri estuary, to examine its position and capabilities as a port for country craft. The late Lord Gifford, who was then travelling in India, came with him, and we took soundings on the bar at mean tide, finding, if I remember right, fourteen feet of water, or depth quite sufficient to admit small vessels. But nothing would move the merchants from Coompta.

The falls of Gairsappa have long been justly reputed one of the sights of the world; for here a very considerable river which divides North Canara from Mysore falls from the tableland over a precipice of a thousand feet into a wild and beautiful ravine.

The road to the falls from Sirci passes for two stages along the brow of the ghauts, mostly through forest. But this is not one of the broad thoroughfares cut with Roman directness through the woods, like the roads which lead coastward; it is a mere woodland path, and crosses all the streams which make their way down the ghaut. Of these, two or three are of such breadth and volume as to necessitate foot-bridges, and as two or even three spans are needed, at least two piers have to be built. Masonry would be too costly and difficult, and in its place native resource has devised a kind of pier which, so long as its materials remain undecayed, answers admirably. Circular crates of about six feet in diameter and height are made by working long tough lianas between cross staves, hurdle-wise; these are placed in position and filled with great stones taken from the bed of the torrent, and out of the centre of the stones rise two strong uprights, connected at intervals by cross pieces. On the topmost cross piece (of about two feet wide) rests the footway, formed of poles lashed together, side rails are added, and as the footway is ten or twelve feet above the bed of the stream, a sort of inclined plane or ladder gives access to it from each bank of the river. Horses must cross these streams as best they may when the water is low. At flood time they had better stay at home.

Long before the traveller reaches the scene the thunder of falling waters is in his ears, and he catches distant glimpses of the white cloud which hovers in the ravine. When the river is brimful from bank to bank, and its entire volume is rolling over the precipice in one vast wave, there is really little to be seen, because the clouds so fill the whole ravine as to shroud the scene. But when the time of high flood has passed, the waters are found to have parted into four divisions, each of which as it passes over the brink of the precipice assumes an individual character totally unlike the rest, just as four members of one family may be found differing so strikingly in face and form and temper, as to make their common origin matter of surprise.

In this family there is one plain and

unamiable member, called the "Roarer," who reminds one of a mad giant escaped from Bedlam. He has ground and torn the face of the rock in his downward course, and is for ever frantically striving to shatter it further. The other three wear forms of exquisite beauty. The head of the family, called "The Great Fall," makes one deliberate plunge of a thousand feet, unbroken by contact, and falling into a basin which has been sounded for three hundred feet without a bottom being reached. This matchless column occupies a semi-circular niche in the precipice, which looks like a shrine hollowed out on purpose.

The other two falls, the "Rocket" and the "Dame Blanche," owe their peculiar characteristics to the form of the rocks they encounter as they leave the verge of the precipice.

The "Rocket" is at once shattered by this contact out of all resemblance to water, seeming to become a cloud of snow, which is fain to descend in successive bouquets of rockets. But in the case of the "Dame Blanche," some stately rock nymph, in human outlines of the fairest, seems to have slipped into her natural and appropriate robes of water lace, so perfect is the illusion of the ever-flowing drapery. A frequent rainbow singles out for special honour this peerless maiden.

Many persons find it impossible to look from so profound a precipice as that over which the river falls at Gairsappa. I have known one visitor who not only found it necessary to lie flat on his face, but had his legs firmly held while he looked over the edge. A good-sized fragment thrown from the summit dwindles to a speck, and finally disappears before it reaches the base; and to any one looking upward from the pools below, men seem like crows upon the top.

When the river is low, it is possible by throwing temporary plank bridges from rock to rock, to reach a ledge of bare rock which projects about ten feet beyond the face of the precipice, midway between the "Dame Blanche" and the "Roarer." Crawling out upon this rugged projection, with nothing but the sky above and the abyss below, the deafening roar of waters in the ears, and the "water smoke" circling round one, the falls may be looked at face to face at very close quarters.

This venture has a strange fascination about it, as I can vouch, having tried it. My wife and another lady insisted on coming too, and we were all three so wound up by the "exaltation" of the situation, that none of the painful promptings which sometimes assail people in such positions came to disturb us.

THE FALLS OF GAIRSAPPA.

Voice of the cataract! Upon the mist
Is borne the thunder of thy stern rebuke.
Where wast thou, mortal, when the hand of God
Quarried yon chasm in the living rock,
And rent the hills to give the torrent way?
How pigmy on the verge thy stature shows,
Set on a rampart of a thousand feet!

Bend o'er the summit as the whirling clouds
Now shroud, now show, the strife of rock and flood
In depths where peace and silence never came.
Yet the blue pigeon circles at mid height,
And in the sprays the darting swallow bathes.

Grudge not the toil to track yon rugged stair,
Down where huge fragments strew the torrent's bed,
Then turn and face the fairest scene on earth.

How goodly are thy robes, thou foam-clad queen,
With hues of heaven woven in thy skirt;
Thy misty veil, how gracefully it falls;
For ever falls, and yet unveils thee not!

What ails thee, O fair stream, that thou art wrought
To fling thyself a snow-cloud on the winds,
Thy substance lost and all thy being changed?
In countless flights thy silent heralds come.
Now errant shoot, now seem to hang in air,
Then quiver down the gloom of the abyss,
And die like meteors in November skies.

Yonder moves one like hero to his doom,
Resolved, serene, not parting from the verge

Or wildly or in haste, sublime of mien,
The noble emblem of a noble end;
For ever set a wonder and a praise,
The highest, goodliest column of the world.

Far other mood is his, yon giant shape,
Borne on reluctant and resisting hurled,
With raving protest, from the precipice.
Rave on, and roll thy rude bulk o'er the rocks,
And be for aye the foil to others' praise!

CHAPTER VII.

A VISIT TO THE HAIGAHS.

ABOUT twenty miles from Belikeri, among the lower slopes of the hills, and in a region where the forest gives place here and there to open grassy hills, were a cluster of villages inhabited by Haigah Brahmins, a race seldom to be met with in Canara, and of whom I have never heard elsewhere. These are the only Brahmins who undertake any kind of manual labour, and even with them it is limited to the cultivation of the gardens in which they grow the arica palm.

I had never seen a Haigah until I undertook an expedition to visit one of their villages under peculiar circumstances. During the rains a death had occurred in this village, regarding which it seemed doubtful whether the deceased, a young man of twenty, had committed suicide by hanging himself in the cowhouse, as reported by his family, or whether a family quarrel had led to an act of vengeance.

There was no evidence forthcoming as to the manner of the death, and it seemed to me that an inspection of the place would at least show whether it was possible for a man to hang himself in the manner described.

I resolved, therefore, to make this inspection in person, and without notice. It was not practicable to take a horse, as the forest streams were sure to be full, and I began the journey in a tonjon; but after travelling about seven miles, we came to an unfordable torrent, the only means of crossing which was a tiny "dugout," of rude construction, and very crank. Here, therefore, I sent back the tonjon, resolving to walk the rest of the way.

Honama and ten or twelve of his shikaries were with me, carrying my baggage, but none of these had skill enough to work the "dugout" to and fro, neither could either of the two peons who accompanied me undertake it.

In this dilemma a man of action came

to the front unexpectedly, in the person of Domingo, my Concani dressing-boy (or valet). He was a shy little fellow, active and intelligent, slim and good-looking, and not in the least like the practised waterman he showed himself. He came forward, examined the canoe, seized the bit of board which was to serve for a paddle, then placing a hand on each side of the stern, he gave the tiny boat a vigorous shoot into the stream, springing from the bank as he did so, and poising his weight on his hands as he curled his legs into the stern; seated there, he shot the canoe across like an arrow, and returning ferried over, in a number of successive trips, everybody and everything belonging to us.

We were delayed too long at this place to attempt to reach our destination that day, and I passed the night rather miserably in the little veranda of a native house, belonging to the *Potail* of a forest hamlet on our way.

Next morning down came the rain, but we found the streams passable, and reached the Haigah village that evening, wet and weary, and much bullied by the tiny jungle leeches which fasten on one's ankles and legs, and sometimes drop from the boughs on to the neck of the passer-by.

The Haigahs installed me in the spacious stone portico of their temple, and neither priest nor layman objected when Domingo brought in a basin of water and bathed my bleeding ankles. There, too, I dined and slept, *tant bien que mal*, owing such comforts as I got to Domingo's resource and activity.

The next day was fine, and I looked out from the temple on a scene of unexpected beauty. I was on the confines of the forest, and all up the sides of the open hills rose, terrace above terrace, the gardens of the Haigahs, and their picturesque *châlets*. Little rills were led through the gardens, and fell from terrace to terrace, and over all this waved groves of the most graceful of the palm family.

I visited the house where the deceased had lived, and saw the rest of the family. I found the Haigahs a frank, manly race, large of limb and fairer than any Hindoos I have seen. I even thought I saw a ruddy tint in the cheeks of the younger men.

They took me at once to the village cowhouse, which was on the border of the pasture land, about a quarter of a mile off, and pointed out the beam from which the poor young fellow was found hanging. First, however, the herdsman drew me away from the door, and placed me behind the corner of the building while he let out the cattle.

This was a necessary precaution, for the herd burst out like a torrent, shaggy half-wild buffaloes of the breed found in Soopah; a stranger standing opposite the door would instantly have been swept away.

It was no pleasant undertaking to make one's way inside this place. I found, however, on examining it, that it would be perfectly easy for a man to stand on the rack which ran along the side of the building, tie a rope to the beam, and swing himself off from the rack. With this presumption in favour of the story of suicide I was forced to be content; I could learn nothing more, and left my Haigah friends as wise as I came.

The arica palm, to which I have here alluded, is cultivated in India, so far as I know, only in the western provinces. It is so valuable and beautiful a member of the palm tribe, and so little known, that a description will not be out of place.

A slender shaft from thirty to forty feet high, and having a diameter at base of no more than six inches, supports a dark green crown of large heavy leaves of more massive appearance than the foliage of the cocoa-nut, the date, or the sago-palm.

During the fruiting season the nuts hang in clusters below the leaves, and enhance the beauty of the effect. As the climber ascends to gather them, the tree sways with his weight, and when he has gathered the ripe nuts he can, by oscillating the stem vigorously from side to side, grasp the leaves of the adjoining tree, and draw himself on to its crown; and thus without the toil of climbing each tree in succession, he visits the whole of the plantation.

The nut of the arica palm, or soopari, as it is called in Hindostani, is known to Europeans as "betel nut," a corruption of "vetelei," which is the Tamil name of the leaf in which the nut is rolled when it is chewed. I need scarcely say that the enormous demand for this nut throughout the East makes the crop very valuable.

Monkeys are fond of the pulp which covers the nut, and as the plantations are generally near the forest, these plunderers often visit and rob the trees. Doleful, and of course exaggerated, complaints of the evil deeds of the monkeys used to be poured into my ears at settlement time by the owners of gardens in forest neighbourhoods; but they had various devices for checkmating the monkeys, and did not lose so much as they pretended.

When the soil and other conditions favoured its cultivation, the cardamom was often grown between the rows of arica trees. No curry is complete without a certain admixture of this spice; so that it is in great demand as a condiment in all parts of India, besides its medicinal value.

The blossom of the plant resembles a gladiolus, and is very beautiful, the white wax-like bells being tinted inside with vermilion and orange.

The manner in which the cardamom is raised in the hill forests of Malabar and on the Anamalie mountains of Coimbatore, seems to involve the vexed question of spontaneous generation. The manner of its growth is as follows: the prospecter for cardamom cultivation selects a forest glade where shade and sunshine are fairly balanced; it must be sheltered and moist, and the trees it grows, must be of the soft-wooded kinds which decay rapidly after they are cut down.

These trees are felled and left to rot on the ground for three years, and at the end of that time the cardamom springs up *unsown*, owing its existence, apparently, simply to certain conditions of soil and climate. I do not venture into the scientific arena, but personally I find no difficulty in believing that the productive energy imparted to the earth under the Divine command to "bring forth" abundantly, is still active under peculiar conditions outside the law which makes the renewal of vegetable life by means of seed the usual rule.

CHAPTER VIII.

THE NILGHERRIES. AN IBEX BEFORE BREAKFAST.

THE Nilgherry hills attain a height of from eight to nine thousand feet, and therefore might fairly claim to be called mountains; but no one accords them that dignified name, because, though here and there rocky peaks and precipitous crags are to be met with, the prevailing aspect of the summits is soft and rounded, and the slopes are green and sweeping. It is a surprise to the traveller who gradually climbs the steep sides of the grand ravine by which Conoor is approached, to find himself emerging from the companionship of woods and crags into an undulating plateau of huge green downs sloping down to broad, saucer-shaped valleys, a land of wild flowers and running streams and scattered coppices.

The plateau extends irregularly for between twenty and thirty miles, with an average breadth of somewhat less, presenting its greatest elevation to the west, from which quarter it is visited by the rains of the south-west monsoon from June to September. During this period the western summits pass much of their time in the clouds, though there occur delicious "breaks in the monsoon," during which the sun makes amends for his frequent absence, and the flowers get quite beyond bounds. The eastern faces of the plateau get their principal rainfall from the north-east monsoon in November, December, and the first week of January, and they enjoy besides whatever the clouds of the south-west monsoon have to spare after deluging the western hills.

Making allowance for an over-liberal amount of rain and wind at certain times, there is not a more beautiful range of country and a more enjoyable climate to be found anywhere in the East than on these hills; and though large game is said to be getting scarce near the three stations where English life chiefly congregates, yet to those who do not shrink from the fatigues of seeking for them, bison, elk, ibex, and of course tigers, leopards, and bears are still to be found; so that a sportsman can still find much to attract him on the Nilgherries. During a hasty visit to the Nilgherries in 1853, I made a special expedition to the haunts of the ibex, an animal I had never yet shot and had only once seen. Ibex are only found on those skirts of the hills, where both the green slopes and the forests which clothe the sides of the plateau give place to crag and precipice. Here grow the herbs they love, and here alone are to be found the perilous homes accessible to none but themselves and the eagles, and in which they find peace and security.

Making inquiries in the proper

quarter, I was introduced to two shikaries who vowed to show me an ibex, and engaged to be ready at daylight next morning to accompany me. The plan was that we should start at daylight from Ootacamund, make straight for a traveller's bungalo on the Pycaroo River, distant twelve miles, breakfast there, and then spend the day among the crags in the company of the ibex. We were to follow the bridle road to Pycaroo, and I chartered a decent pony to carry me there, having brought no horses with me to the hills.

Before we had gone many miles my shikaries began communing together for my benefit. "What a pity to keep to the bridle road, when by striking across the hills we might pass close to an ibex ground and just examine it; who knows but the sahib might get a buck before breakfast!" So the sahib, against his better judgment, forsook the road and took to the hill-sides. The first drawback to this course soon presented itself; a brook at the bottom of one of the long slopes had to be crossed, the hither bank high and broken, but the opposite landing a sward of emerald moss. The width was no great matter, and within the pony's compass; he gathered himself bravely for the leap, and landed well on the centre of the moss,—disappearing up to the withers! the said moss being a moss in a different sense from what I fondly supposed. Such places are common enough on the Nilgherries, but I was not then up to the deception. I scuttled out, and we hauled up the poor pony well coated with black mud. A little farther on, the track led us along the edge of a landslip which had broken away the ground below the path on our left, to the right the hill-side rose smooth and grassy, and on it grazed a herd of half-wild buffaloes of the Toda aborigines. The lodges (or munds) of this singular race are now extremely rare; as not more than five hundred of the tribe survive, they are to be found only in secluded spots, and near them graze the shaggy herds on whose milk they chiefly subsist. These buffaloes are often dangerous to strangers, and when we came in sight the herd galloped wildly down towards us. At ten paces from the path they halted in line, staring at us with their noses in the air. The landslip obliged us to pass close in front of them, and telling my men to follow very quietly, and assuming an indifference I was far from feeling, I moved slowly past the forest of horns and noses, prepared to fire and stampede them if they moved. Fortunately for us not a head was lowered, and as we cleared the phalanx the herdsman ran yelling down the hill, a call which seemed to calm the herd, and they submitted to be driven upward. From this point I sent the mud-cased pony to Pycaroo, and devoted myself to the ibex I was to shoot before breakfast. On and on we prowled along the brows of grand precipices, peering over the edges and creeping stealthily among the clefts. Every new stretch of ground we reached was to be absolutely the last. "We would just look round and then go to breakfast." Noon came, and thoroughly famished I was about to turn, when one of my men actually sighted ibex. Beckoning me to the ledge over which he was gazing, he pointed far far down, half-way to the plains as it seemed to me, and there, on a grassy ledge at the foot of one precipice and on the brow of another, were four or five brown specks, which after much scrutiny resolved themselves into ibex lying down. "How are we to get near them?" I asked; for in truth nothing but a balloon could have carried one either up or down the precipice. "You cannot go down, sahib; but at about two o'clock the ibex will feed slowly upwards, and we can take you to a spot where they will come within shot."

Relinquishing all hopes of breakfast, I sat down in the spot pointed out to me, to wait the ascent of the ibex, while my guides went on to watch an alternative position. Never did two hours seem so interminable; but at last, on a rock about sixty paces below me, there suddenly and without warning stood, like an apparition, an ibex and her kid. As the pretty creature paused for a moment and looked about her, I fired; the ibex bounded into the air and disappeared utterly. I saw nothing more of her, and was resigning myself to disappointment, when on the very same rock, and standing just as the doe had stood, there appeared a buck! My first had been a steady, careful shot, and now, resting the gun on a rock, I fired my second barrel with still greater care. Again there was an upward bound, and the buck was gone! This was too grievous, but just then came a shout from below, and the shikaries announced that they had seen the buck when I fired, and that he had fallen into a ravine. Down they went accordingly, nothing daunted, and after a scramble lasting about half an hour, they brought me up the head of the buck (which carried a handsome pair of horns) and a hind quarter. The shikaries had been watching another point when my first shot was fired, and had not seen what became of the doe. I reached Pycaroo by four o'clock in the afternoon, exhausted but happy.

The next day was devoted to elk stalking in a different direction, and amidst very different scenery. Truly the elk had there a glorious region for their wanderings, and I longed to enclose a park of a few square miles in situations where interminable stretches of green lawn descended far away towards the plains, flanked on either side by stately woods. In other places the skirt of heavy forest was drawn higher up the slopes of the hills, or even invaded the upper plateau; and sometimes isolated woods and winding open glades divided the land equally between them, interlapping like fiord and headland.

After wandering all the forenoon among these fair scenes, shooting a young elk and seeing others at intervals, I lunched, and sat down on a hill-side to watch the outskirts of a wood about four hundred yards below me, where elk were known to harbour. At four o'clock, if an elk was in the wood he would be sure to come out to graze.

The slope of the hill on which I sat did not descend evenly, but ended in three or four knolls separated by corresponding depressions, thus breaking the outline of the ground where it skirted the wood; there the grass grew tall and rank almost breast high, but on the hill-side it was short.

My companions had withdrawn, to watch another point, they said, but I rather think they went to sleep, for when at four o'clock a noble stag which had been lying down in the long grass near the wood rose out of one of the depressions and stretched himself, no one saw him but myself.

I instantly sank down flat and drew myself out of his ken. My plan of action was obvious. I could lower myself on my back down the hill to the skirt of the wood without coming into view; there would then be three little knolls and hollows between me and the stag, and as I crawled up the brow of the third knoll, I should be within thirty yards. When I reached the bottom of the hill, I took to my hands and knees, and crept painfully on. As I mounted the third and last slope, I became conscious that my hands were getting unsteadied; but my calculations had been exact, and as I cautiously rose to my knees I saw right in front of me, through the grass, the outlines of a pair of round ears and a dark muzzle. The elk was taking stock of me, and not a moment was to be lost; so without rising higher, and steadying myself by a desperate effort, I aimed through the nodding grass-tops, six inches below the nose of the elk, in a line to reach the throat. There was a rush, and I started to my feet; the elk was off, but at about seventy yards he stopped and turned his side to me. I raised the rifle for a fatal shot.

To my amazement and disgust all power of control was gone from me; the muzzle of the gun waved wildly to and fro. I could not cover him, and fired I knew not where. Away went the elk, but rather slowly, and just then the two shikaries came over the brow where he disappeared. "Run, sahib, run!" they shouted; "the elk is lying down just over the hill." I started to run, but the rebellion in the camp was not confined to my hands and arms, my legs *would* not run, I could barely compel them to a slow jog-trot. However, we followed the wounded stag along the Pycaroo river, tracking him by the blood for some miles, till we approached a little wood by the river side, and saw on the hill beyond it some hill-men running down to us. The elk was in the wood, they said; so we formed line and searched it through and through, but without success. It grew dark, and the shikaries declared that the stag must have lain down in the river, leaving only his nostrils clear of the surface, this being a known way of concealment practised by wounded elk. After this there was nothing for it but to grope our way back to Pycaroo, and next morning I was obliged to return. The elk I shot looked near fourteen hands high, but his horns were in the velvet.

A dear friend of mine, now dead,

a keen sportsman and as fine a fellow as ever stepped, told me that when elk-stalking in the same neighbourhood (possibly in the same spot), he had seen from the hill a large animal moving in the grass, which he took to be an elk, and which he proceeded to stalk much as I had done. He too crawled through the long grass and raised his head as he drew near his game, and then saw in front of him no elk, but the great round face of a tiger. He only had with him a light single-barrelled rifle, and it would have been madness to fire; so he at once dropped and drew quietly backwards. "I thought the brute would hear my heart beating, it made such a row," he told me. His friend watching his movements from the hill-side, saw that something was wrong, and came running down; and when he looked up again the tiger had disappeared.

On another day the same two companions in search of elk as before, again ascended a hill-side and sat down to watch the wood below, through which they had just passed.

They had not watched long when just at the point where they quitted the wood there emerged not an elk but a tiger; he came out with his nose to the ground and began ascending the hill, still sniffing on the exact line they had followed. They watched the brute with indignant and unpleasant surprise. Could he be stalking them?

This soon became no longer doubtful, so they took counsel and mounted into the branches of a small tree near at hand, agreeing that when the tiger reached a certain point A. should fire, B. keeping his gun in reserve. The tiger continued slowly to mount the hill towards them; and as they sat and watched him the suspense grew more and more trying. At last the man who was to have reserved his shot could stand it no longer, and fired, missing the tiger altogether! But the shot had the effect of leading the tiger to reconsider the matter; he looked about him, roared, and finally turned and went down the hill again. And so ended a rather exciting afternoon

Among the rather numerous enemies of the elk, the wild dog holds a foremost place. A pack of wild dogs hunts down game just as a pack of staghounds would do, following the scent staunchly to the end. These dogs correspond to the coyotes of South America, and are dreaded by every beast of the forest, not excepting the tiger. They do not attack man, but would probably resent his interference with their proceedings. The colour is always a fox-like red, and the size and shape are those of a slightly built foxhound, but the muzzle is sharp, and the ears erect. My friend Mr. Ward assured me that the wild dog stands in awe of his domestic brother, and that a pointer of his ran into the midst of a pack, was received with deference, and kidnapped a puppy unmolested.

I once fell in with a pack of wild dogs not far from Pycaroo, as I was riding to Sispara. Apparently they had just concluded a run, as they were lying at ease on the sward outside a wood. I cantered up to the pack in order that I might see the wild dogs more closely. They did not run off as I expected, but rose lazily, and moved but a short distance. When I returned to the bridle road, four of the dogs rose and trotted after me, sniffing at my horse's heels. On one side of the scarped path the hill rose steeply, and when one of the dogs leaped up the bank, and trotted alongside me, he was on a level with my saddle, and not three paces off. I thought it necessary to draw my hunting-knife, and hold it between me and this inquisitive dog, as I did not half like these attentions. I kept the horse at a walk, lest they should fancy he was a beast of the chase, and so we went on for about a hundred yards, to a point where a small stream crossed the track. Here the dogs began lapping the water, and lay down in it, nor did they follow me any further; probably they never meant to do so, but their familiarity, so different from the habits of wolf or jackal, struck me as very strange. Perhaps some latent instinct attracts them to man, and to those of their own race whom he has made his friends and companions.

In speaking of the wild animals

which are to be found on the Nilgherries, I must not omit the elephant; but elephants wander far and wide, and they are but casual visitors on the higher slopes. Some years ago, Mr. Wedderburn, a member of the Madras service, lost his life when elephant shooting on these hills; he was watching from his concealment the movements of an elephant he had wounded, and fancying that he could reach a better position unperceived, left his place and moved across. He was instantly seen and chased; the ground was rough, and as he ran he stumbled and fell, and was at once overtaken by the elephant and killed.

In the deep forest which lies between the western face of the Nilgherries and the town and port of Calicut, elephants are often found, and at one time travellers on the road leading from Calicut to the Sispara ghaut, which ascends the hills on that side, were exposed to interruption from this cause.

A friend of mine travelling with his wife and his servant along this road had a very hazardous meeting with a rogue elephant near the foot of the ghaut.

The party travelled in palanquins, carried by bearers in the usual Indian fashion. On a sudden there was a cry of alarm, and the bearers, dropping their burdens, dashed into the jungle.

Mr. M—— had just time to drag his wife behind the trees when the angry tusker reached the spot. Fortunately the brute was so much interested in the palanquins that he did not concern himself about the fugitives; his anger appeared to concentrate itself on Mr. M——'s palanquin. He overthrew it, crushed it, tore it open, and finally stamped upon it so perseveringly that scarcely a bit of it over the size of a plate was left unbroken. Having thus vindicated his seignorial rights, the elephant departed as he had come.

Next day a party of shikaries started to exterminate this elephant, and bands of woodcutters cleared away the underwood for ten or twenty paces on the margin of the track, so that when, a fortnight later, my wife and I traversed the same forest, we were assured the road was safe. Nevertheless, on the lower part of the ghaut,* we came on fresh traces of an elephant, and I walked the whole way with my gun on my shoulder.

---

* This ghaut has been disused for some years.

CHAPTER IX.

GANJAM.

THE province of Ganjam extends along the Coromandel coast from Calingapatam to the confines of Orissa; it lies between the sea and the Khond and Sourah hills, and is peopled partly by Teloogoos and partly by Ooriyahs. The ancient kingdom of Orissa once included the whole of Ganjam as far south as Calingapatam, but the Ooriyah population were thrust back from the sea-coast and the open plains adjoining it by a stronger race than themselves, and they now inhabit the semi-forest region skirting the hills, and cultivate the lands of some eight or ten zemindari estates, the appanages of ancient Ooriyah families.

The Teloogoos are a strong and manly race, differing from the Ooriyahs much as the Germans differ from the French; they are ryots holding their lands direct from the British Government.

In times still more remote, the Ooriyahs must have dispossessed and driven into the hills the Khond and Sourah tribes who now inhabit them. Where these races are in contact with the Ooriyah zemindaries, they acknowledge a sort of fealty to the zemindar, but this authority is of a vague character, and does not extend far, and except in so far as the British Government has interfered to suppress human sacrifice, female infanticide, and crimes of violence, Khonds and Sourahs are left very much to themselves.

These two aboriginal races have nothing in common, and keep apart from each other. The Sourahs are short, wiry men, of fair complexion, fierce, cunning, and inclined to robbery; the Khonds are a dark-skinned race of gentler nature, much addicted to carrying formidable-looking weapons, but not prompt to use them. They carry on their tribal feuds in a slow, ceremonious, Homeric fashion, and are by no means bloodthirsty.

There is not a single trait, physical, social, or religious, to connect either of these aboriginal tribes with the Hindoos, nor is there any affinity of language; the hillmen visit the bazaars and markets of the low country, bringing down turmeric and taking back cattle, cloth, and brass ware, but there is no disposition on either side for further intercourse.

One curious evidence of former dispossession and uprooting is to be found in the Khond ignorance of the uses of milk; they have now acquired cattle, and they breed them and use them both for the plough and for food, *but they never attempt to milk their cows.* Probably when they were driven from their ancient seats they were stripped of everything, and remained for generations without cattle.

Tobacco grows round every village in these hills, and the Khonds smoke it from their earliest childhood, and stick their pipes and half-smoked cheroots in their matted hair, having no other pocket available. The Sourah, however, as far as I observed, prefers to use his tobacco in the form of snuff. Every man of them carries somewhere about him a tiny snuff-box, shaped like a humming-top, and made from the rind of the wood-apple; it contains pale, high-dried snuff, made from the baked stalk of the leaf, and is very strong. There can be little doubt that the free use of tobacco in the feverish valleys of the Khond plateau is a preservative from fever and ague.

The weapons of these tribes are the

bow and arrow, a long-handled, formidable-looking battle-axe, and the quarter-staff. Their Ooriyah neighbours possess fire-arms and manufacture gunpowder. West of the Khond highlands lie the wild forests of Bustar and Kharonde, inhabited by the Gond race. In very many Khond villages two or three families of Gonds are to be found. They are the potters and weavers of the community, and their position among the Khonds seems to suggest that they may have been detained in order to render these services while others of their race were driven westward to the deeper forests by the Khonds when they themselves retired before the Ooriyahs.

The Gond hand-loom and its productions are of the rudest description, and many of the Gonds of the Kharonde and Bustar forests are entirely without clothing. Their pottery, however, is often prettily shaped, being evidently moulded on the pattern of the bottle-gourd, that curious natural exemplar which seems to have been specially formed for the instruction of the potter. These gourds, which are produced in endless variety of proportion, from the flat-bodied, long-necked goblet to the capacious bottle with mouthpiece of suitable length, are common in the Khond villages, and the potters imitate their outlines.

The history of the successive races which have inhabited Ganjam is thus a mere repetition of what has occurred in many other countries, the weakest everywhere giving way to the more civilised and powerful; and the case is only so far exceptional that the steps of the process are still so plainly discernible, and that the different races, though in juxta-position, have not amalgamated as in European countries. Teloogoo and Ooriyah, Khond, Sourah and Gond, remain as distinct from each other as at the first; and the same separation obtains throughout Central India in the case of the Gonds of the Nerbudda valley, the Bheels and other aboriginal tribes.

I took charge of the district of Ganjam in 1858, and a year or two later the special agency for the suppression of human sacrifices and infanticide among the Khonds was added to my duties. This involved a yearly visit to the hill region, and brought with it opportunities of closer acquaintance with its inhabitants.

Apart from these special sources of interest, Ganjam contained much that was worthy of note, and a residence of nine years in the district (including a temporary absence in England) has induced me to devote the following chapters to recording such portions of my experience there as are likely to be of general interest.

The hill ranges, of which I have spoken, give the district a very irregular border on its western side. They recede from the coast to a distance of seventy or eighty miles at the northern and southern extremities, and advance to within twenty miles of the sea towards the centre, where the great detached mountain, known in ancient Hindoo story as Mahendragiri, attains a height of nearly five thousand feet, and flanks the plain for a distance of twenty miles. Another extensive cluster of hills projects from the main range to the north of Mahendra, and approaches within fifteen miles of the sea. A few Khond villages are scattered among these last named hills, which are almost isolated from the rest of the Khond highlands, and are surrounded by the cultivated lands of the Ooriyah villages. The Teloogoo population ceases at about this point, and gives place to the Ooriyah Zemindaries, which extend northward and westward as far as the borders of the beautiful Chilka Lake, which separates Ganjam from Cuttack and Pooree (or Jugganath).

CHAPTER X.

THE CHILKA.

THE Chilka Lake extends from Pooree to the neighbourhood of the town of Ganjam, a distance of nearly fifty miles, with an average width of ten miles. It is separated from the sea by a narrow sandy plain, but is bordered on its inland side by a varied and beautiful margin of hill and woodland. The lake is fed by a branch of the Mahanuddi (which joins the sea near Pooree), and during the rains its surplus waters cut their way to the sea at the narrowest point of the intervening plain, by a channel which remains open to the tide for the greater part of the year.

Thus the Chilka is neither wholly salt nor wholly fresh; but it is full of fish, produces immense quantities of prawns, and is in consequence the resort of great numbers of wild fowl. Pelicans and cormorants of different sorts fish its waters, and waders of all sizes and species feed along its shores. The osprey and the fish hawk are always to be seen there, and vast flocks of wild duck and teal of many varieties make it their favourite haunt.

Among the rocks at the base of the hills which here and there descend into the lake, colonies of otters find a congenial home, and where there is space for a margin of green turf, the peafowl steals out from among the overhanging bamboo clumps, morning and evening, to pick up small marine insects.

Several islands are scattered about the lake, some flat and rush-grown, where water-rail and teal, and some other species breed, and where collectors of eggs may find specimens not often procurable. But the most remarkable of the group is Bird Island, a high pile of boulders at the southern end of the lake, and distant about two miles from the shore. It is greatly favoured by birds of many sorts as a breeding-place. Even birds which usually build on the mainland, like the osprey and the common blue pigeon, seem to prefer the security and solitude of the lonely island.

There is an osprey's nest on the stunted tree which has rooted itself among the boulders on the top of the pile, and among the multitude of birds of all sorts which rise from the rocks and darken the air when a gun is fired, the intrusive blue pigeon is conspicuous.

If a boat approaches Bird Island quietly, the representatives of many families may be seen on their nests between or under the rocks: the heron and the crested heron, the white egret and the black water-crow or cormorant, and the snake bird, a larger kind of cormorant, so called because only the snake-like neck and head are visible above water as the bird swims. The grave, awkward-looking and helpless young of the pelican are to be seen squatted on a flat rock five or six feet above the water, from which it would be easy for the parent bird to push them down into the lake. I have also seen flamingoes and other cranes on the island, but I do not think they breed there.

We collected many kinds of eggs among the rocks, the prevailing colour among them was a pale bluish green, and the shape an elongated and pointed oval; some four eggs only were white. A pair of young crested herons, nearly full fledged, were also carried off on one of our visits, and for a time throve upon the fish we gave them. They were very pugnacious birds, and full of life; but they came at last to an untimely end, I think from over-eating.

The lee side only of Bird Island is in favour with the birds, none are to be seen in the quarter exposed to the south-west monsoon.

A quarter of a mile from the western shore of the Chilka is Deer Island, a low sandy islet, almost covered with thicket, except along its shores, where the rise and fall of tidal water only permits the growth of a wide margin of saline turf. There are glades here and there among the underwood and a few trees. The whole length of the little island is less than a mile. This is the chosen haunt of a small herd of spotted deer, which seems to cross at pleasure from the mainland, some of them being almost always to be found on "Deer Island." If the covert is beaten with great care and perseverance, beginning from the northern end, it is sometimes possible to get a shot when the deer double back on the beaters along the open margin; but the underwood is so dense, and the deer show so much cunning in creeping on their knees under thickets or lying resolutely hidden in impenetrable brakes, that small as is the area of Deer Island, it affords a fairly secure retreat to its inhabitants.

I often observed alligators in the channel between the island and the mainland, probably they were able occasionally to seize a deer as the herd crosses.

The sandy plain which separates the

Chilka Lake from the sea is not more than two miles wide, and it becomes gradually narrower towards the spot where the lake is open to the sea. Considerable herds of antelope graze over this plain, which is in parts thinly clothed with grass, and they may be stalked and coursed there. On one occasion a deer drive of a singular kind occurred on this narrow spit of land. The 5th Regiment Native Infantry was on the march from Ganjam to Pooree, and as the cholera prevailed along the high road west of the lake, the regiment marched along its eastern side. The antelope retired as the troops advanced, accumulating before them in an increasing multitude. Finding the spit narrowing, the commanding officer formed the regiment in single line across it, so as at last to cover the entire width, and thus the antelope were enclosed between the lake, the sea, and the advancing line. Gradually forced towards the water, the herd suddenly stopped, turned, and rushing straight at the line, bounded clean over the men's heads and broke away.

Over the safe and tranquil water way, afforded by the Chilka Lake, a constant traffic is kept up between Pooree and Rhumba, a small town at the Ganjam end of the lake. The rice grown in Ganjam is of a finer sort than that produced on the delta lands of the Mahánuddi near Pooree, and is more in demand for the European export trade; consequently the thrifty ryots of Ganjam furnish exporters with their own produce at remunerative prices, and themselves consume the cheaper grain brought from Pooree to Rhumba on the Chilka boats.

There, too, is landed a good deal of oil-cake, not destined, as might be supposed, to fatten cattle, but to be used as manure on the plots where sugar-cane is cultivated. Richly manured land and nine months' supply of water are needed for the sugar crop, of which a good deal is raised in Ganjam, and for this, oil-cake manure is highly esteemed.

The boats used on the lake are curiosities in their way. Seen at a little distance the rise of the gunwale outline at stem and stern gives these craft an antique and classic look, but closer examination shows them to be mere oblong boxes, with flat bottom and flat perpendicular sides, about six feet wide by thirty or thirty-five feet long. They are of about ten tons burden, and are very strongly built of sal wood planks an inch and a half thick. As the lake is of nearly uniform depth throughout and has seldom more than two fathoms of water, it is everywhere possible to pole these boats. A stout plank runs along each gunwale, and three or even four men pole on each side, sending the heavy craft at a fair pace through the water. But when the wind is aft two great bamboos are reared, one on each side of the boat, between which is stretched a rude mat, strengthened by cross-pieces, and under this primitive arrangement the voyage continues and the polers take their ease.

The stern of the boat has a deck of split bamboo laths, and is covered by a tilt awning of matwork. With a mattress spread on the laths under the awning it is possible to traverse the lake in all directions and examine its beautiful coves at one's ease, surprising a peafowl here and there, or getting a shot at a basking alligator. For wild duck shooting a canoe is a better craft.

CHAPTER XI.

RHUMBA.

NEAR the town of Rhumba, on a park-like slope which rises gently from the southern shore of the lake, stands a large two-storied house, built at the beginning of this century by a Mr. S——, who was then collector of Ganjam. It is well and strongly built of hewn stone, with extensive offices, and stabling for twenty-four horses, besides elephant stalls; the floors were originally of grey marble, and the fittings of the interior were as perfect as the best workmen specially summoned from Calcutta could make them. Here Mr. S—— passed his days in great luxury, with his house always full of guests, his stable full of horses, and his yacht on the lake. His district establishment was located at Ganjam, nine miles off, and his head official appeared only once a week for the transaction of business.

Very little revenue from Ganjam found its way to the seat of Government in those days, and very evil reports of Mr. S——'s administration reached Madras. Reproofs and warnings came at last in quick succession, with urgent orders for the submission of his long-delayed accounts. Then

Mr. S—— loaded his yacht with the district accounts, ran her on a rock, and reported to his Government the lamentable accident which had deposited the district accounts at the bottom of the lake while he was crossing it for purposes of business.

It was resolved to make an example of Mr. S——; he was dismissed from his post, and desired to give over the charge of the district and treasury to an officer, who was appointed to succeed him, and was charged to make full report of what had passed. But the land journey from Madras was seven hundred miles, and the only mode of travelling was by palanquin and bearers, so that three weeks were required to bring Mr. S——'s successor to the spot;

and though in due course he appeared and claimed to be put in charge, the man in possession calmly ignored him, and he was obliged to report that he had failed to assert his authority. At last means were found to coerce Mr. S—— and lay bare his evil deeds; it then appeared that he had largely misappropriated public money, and in particular that he had built his house at Rhumba with the funds allotted for the employment of starving people during a famine.

The Court of Directors dismissed him from their service, refused him his pension, and caused the Rhumba house to be sold by public auction. There were no bidders, and a Madras firm owning the Aska sugar works bought for £150 a property on which £20,000 had been laid out.

Such is the history of the large and well-planned house which still stands in a beautiful site on the green margin of the Chilka and looks out on the varied beauty of its shores. It is now the property of my friend Mr. Minchin, into whose hands the Aska factory has passed, and who keeps it in good repair. The sequel to Mr. S——'s history is, that after hanging about the India Office in rags for a long time, he obtained the restoration of his pension, drove down with four horses next day to return thanks to the Court, and was soon afterwards run over by a hackney coach and killed.

The firm into whose possession the

house at Rhumba had passed very liberally permitted the district officers and even travellers to make use of it; and whenever there was work to be done in that neighbourhood, or the offices were closed during holidays, a visit to the Chilka Lake was a favourite resource.

The grounds round the house included about a hundred acres, much overgrown with underwood, and here a few spotted deer sometimes harboured. At night bears often passed near the house, and probably other wild creatures also.

One morning, while we were at Rhumba, the wing of a regiment on the march arrived, and the four officers who accompanied it became our guests for that and the following day. It was very hot weather, and the camp cots of our visitors were ranged along the open veranda at the back of the house on the ground floor, a few steps descended from this veranda into the open air, so that it was perfectly accessible from outside.

I was restless that night, and soon after midnight got up and walked about the veranda above where my guests were sleeping. As I looked out into the moonlight I presently perceived two bears moving among the bushes and slowly approaching the house, foraging in the dry grass as they came for white ants and beetles. My gun was at hand; should I use it, or try and rouse the sleepers noiselessly for a shot? but I despaired of doing this without scaring the bears, and again, if I wounded a bear they might start up and run the risk of being attacked. So I called my wife, and for ten minutes we watched the bears as they sauntered to and fro snuffling and scratching the ground, until they slowly passed out of sight unharmed and harming no one.

Next day I took our visitors across a part of the lake to Deer Island, which is about three or four miles from the house. We beat the covert, and were fortunate enough to make the deer break on to the open margin, and to get one of them.

Riding out through the jungle one morning during a subsequent visit to Rhumba, I came suddenly upon a sight which greatly surprised and interested me: seven or eight little conical gipsy tents were pitched in an open glade, constituting evidently only a temporary encampment. In front of each hut stood tethered and picketed like a horse, a black buck antelope. I stopped and inquired from my gipsy friends what this meant, and what manner of men they were. "We are stone-cutters by profession," they said, "and snarers of all kinds of game; and these antelopes are not as the sahib supposes, either pets or intended to be killed and eaten; we use them in capturing other antelope, and we will show the sahib how it is done if he likes."

It is scarcely necessary to say that I caught at the offer, and arranged to have a large boat ready next morning to convey two of the bucks and some of the men across the lake to the sandy plain near the sea, where antelope abounded. The antelopes and their owners were accordingly shipped next morning, and we made our way across the lake. I noticed that with the bucks was brought on board a supply of the flower buds of the white *Asclepias gigantea*, which have very stimulating properties, and are sometimes given in attacks of cholera. The bucks from time to time had a handful of the buds given them, which they ate greedily. The gipsies also brought with them a quantity of very tough but fine cord, intended for the fighting harness of the antelopes.

The approach from the lake to the

sandy plain, which separates it from the sea, is through a labyrinth of little channels, winding between green mounds. The prevailing southerly and south-westerly winds are for ever intruding sandy banks and hillocks into the Chilka, and these soon become grass-covered and fixed.

Under cover of these banks and mounds, we landed within a quarter of a mile of a large herd of antelope, and one of our champions was forthwith accoutred for the coming encounter. Running nooses of cord hung from the base of the horns, and others over the shoulders, and then the ends of the cord were brought farther back and wound round the buck at the girth. He was then set free, and at once trotted gently towards the herd. As he drew near, the antelopes ceased feeding and raised their heads to observe him, and he then continued his approach at a walk, with his head up, and his nostrils curled back after the manner of his kind.

The leading buck of the herd at once advanced to meet the intruder, and the two proceeded to move warily on, not facing each other, but following converging lines, which brought them at last within ten paces. Then with a sudden and simultaneous impulse they turned and dashed at each other. For some seconds there was a great clashing of horns as they butted and thrust and parried; but presently both drew back by common consent to take breath for a fresh charge. At the second encounter, and almost as soon as they met, the wild buck got one of his horns caught in the noose, and taking alarm, instantly struggled to escape. His captor simply hung back, allowing himself to be dragged slowly on, while two of his human allies, running up at headlong speed, seized the ensnared buck, threw him down, and lashing one horn to his haunch, shouldered him, and brought him back in triumph.

If I recollect right, my gipsy friends told me that bucks captured full grown could be easily trained to assist in this way in snaring their fellows. This is not quite so strange as it may appear. The antelope is easily tamed, and becomes very familiar and fond of his master, and his combative propensities are strong enough to make it certain that when he is brought near a wild herd he will presently be engaged with one of the bucks; all the rest is simply mechanical. He naturally resists being dragged away by his entangled adversary, and so delivers him into the hands of his captors.

About a hundred yards behind the house at Rhumba, I had noted not far from the approach a landrail's nest of four eggs, *a nest* only by courtesy, as the rail lays her eggs on the bare ground in the open, caring only that the colouring of the soil shall match the dusky reddish-brown of the eggs. But other eyes besides mine had noted the landrail's treasure. I was attracted to the window one day by a great clamour among the landrails, and saw that about a dozen of them were in close attendance upon a large cobra, which was moving slowly straight towards the eggs (a delicacy of which snakes are fond). The rails tried all they knew to stop the cobra or draw him away from the nest. They swooped one after another at his head, almost striking him with their wings, while three or four of them alighted and danced in front of him with outspread wings like children holding out their skirts in a quadrille. The cobra now and then raised his crested head and made a show of striking at one or another, but not in the least did he deviate from his course. At last as he was nearing the nest, I ran out with a gun and put an end to him and his proceedings.

The next day a fresh clamour drew my attention to the landrail's nest; this time a number of the birds were wheeling round the head of a little grey fox who was approaching the spot. He too was going straight for his point, though why, if he knew of the position of the eggs, he had not already eaten them I do not understand, unless the same spot is chosen year after year by the same birds.

Of course the fox took no heed of the remonstrances which assailed him, and I had again to interfere and drive off the enemy, though I did not like to shoot him. Perhaps if I had done so the eggs might have been hatched, but they disappeared in the course of the following day. It is worthy of note that the whole of the flock of landrails interested themselves as much as the parent birds in protecting the eggs.

Coasting along the shores of the lake one afternoon I surprised and killed a large alligator; and, as he was rather a fine specimen, he was tied behind the boat and towed home in order that his head might be preserved. When the alligator was opened a great number of wild duck were found in his inside, feathers and all, just as he had swallowed them. I was rather surprised at first that an alligator should have been able to seize duck; but he would only have to swim quietly along six inches or so below the surface and pull the bird under by the legs without showing himself or alarming the rest of the flock.

I close here my brief notice of the Chilka Lake. It is the largest example of the effect of forces which are in operation all along the Coromandel coast. There is not to be found a single stretch of shingle beach between Cape Comorin and the mouth of the Hoogly; the coast line is everywhere sandy and flat, and the prevailing set of the sea during many months of the year piles the sand along it to a uniform height, forming a barrier through which the rivers cut their way only so long as they maintain a current of sufficient volume to sweep away the sand thrown up by the surf. When the flow in the river-bed is insignificant the bar is closed by a sandy beach, and backwaters are formed parallel to the shore wherever the level of the adjacent land invites the overflow of river water. There are consequently many lagoons of varying size along the twelve hundred miles of coast between Pooree and Cape Comorin, all owing their existence to the same causes which, favoured by exceptional conditions in Ganjam, have pent up in the depression between the hills and the sea-shore the beautiful lake which from the shape of its outline has received the name of the Chilka or Parrot.

It has often been proposed to utilize these backwaters by uniting them so as to form a canal, and a beginning has actually been made; but before an uninterrupted inland water-way can be perfected along the entire coast, means must be found to carry the canal across the river-beds, which during many months interpose at intervals a stretch of dry sand. A canal now unites the Chilka Lake with the mouth of the Ganjam River. It was dug as a famine-relief work during the last year of my administration in Ganjam, in 1867, and if means could be found to contrive a water-way across the river during the dry season it could easily be continued through an intermediate back-water to Gopulpore, a port of call for the steamers of the British India Steam Navigation Company.

CHAPTER XII.

CHETTERPUR.

The head-quarter station of the district was moved many years ago from the town of Ganjam to a breezy upland four miles off, called Chetterpur. A fever of a particularly malignant character had shown itself for two or three years in succession in the once thriving and populous town of Ganjam, and it had become almost depopulated by death and desertion.

The fever has long since disappeared, and the place no longer retains any traces of its time of calamity except in the locality occupied by the fort and the houses of the European officers. This was a pretty green sward with the fort on its seaward face, and several large and well-built houses grouped round it; only two of these remain, surviving in that state of long-protracted decay which is often the lot of the strongest constitutions and the most solid buildings. The fort is sharing the same fate.

Meanwhile, Chetterpur has taken the place of Ganjam as the head-quarters of the Revenue and Magisterial establishments, and the courts of justice have been located at Berhampur, the military cantonment twelve miles off. The country between these places is disposed in great undulating plains, wild and little cultivated; and on the rise of the last of these undulations stands the house of Chetterpur, facing the sea at a distance of three or four miles. A miniature lake, half a mile wide, and extending three miles northward to the Ganjam River, lies at the foot of the slope, and beyond it a plain of sand two miles wide stretches to the sea beach. A sheet of water of this size is called in Ganjam a "tumpra." The one at Chetterpur is one of those lagoons of which I have spoken, formed by the accumulations of sand which close the mouths of the rivers and also hold back the surface drainage from the sea. Wild duck and teal seldom resorted to this tumpra, but I have shot pelican there, and often seen the osprey and the fish-hawk at work. Jackals and hyænas occasionally lurked among the pandanus thickets on the shore, and the little lake had a sullen, dreary aspect, quite in keeping with such company.

Behind the house lay the cultivated fields of the village, screened by dense pandanus hedges from the southerly winds, which were quite capable of carrying away the surface soil bodily in dry weather had it not been for this protection. Still farther to the rear were many miles of rolling plains, partly sand strewn, partly covered with scrub; here there was excellent fox coursing, and here I once or twice met and tried to run down wolves, but without success, as greyhounds very wisely shrink from closing with so formidable a beast.

A shikari one day brought in from these plains the skins of a pair of these animals, both of which he had shot while they were dragging off a calf. He killed one wolf, and found that its companion, instead of running away, continued its attack upon the calf, so that he had time to load again and shoot it also.

From the same wild plains a shepherd brought me a large python which had seized a kid, and which he had killed with a heavy quarter staff, beating it down when it reared itself up at him, and breaking the spine, much as we had killed the python at Belikeri in Canara.

Snakes of many other kinds abounded at Chetterpur, and were frequently killed in or about the house. A snake of some size escaped from under my wife's chair as we were sitting down to dinner one evening, and another dropped almost upon her from the top of a door.

I met a large cobra in the grounds at dusk one evening, which, instead of avoiding me as I expected, made a rush at my feet, and when I sprang to one side again made a similar demonstration. I was so surprised at this unusual conduct that I at first made no attack on the creature; but when I saw it begin to lower itself into the opening of a white ants' nest, from which it had driven me, I understood the reason of its movements, and as soon as its head was underground I struck it heavily across the body and killed it; had the evening been a little darker I should certainly have been bitten.

In some parts of Ganjam a great deal of sugar-cane is grown, and as there are many rocky hills which afford comfortable homes for the bears which abound in the district, circumstances greatly favour these creatures in the gratification of their love of sugar. If they once get through the fence which protects a plot of cane, they can rob and then retire with impunity before daylight to dens, out of which it is often impossible to force them. I have heard of as many as twenty-five bears being seen by one observer in the course of a moonlight night among the cane gardens. A friend of mine once wounded a bear in that neighbourhood and followed it to its den under the rocks. Many unsuccessful attempts were made to dislodge the bear, but at last it occurred to some one to make a lay figure and lower it from the rocks above into the very mouth of the den; there by means of a rope round its waist the dummy was made to dance in so irritating a manner that the bear rushed out at it and was shot.

Near the village of Chetterpur, where there was no other inducement to attract bears than a cluster of rocky hills containing some convenient holes and caves usually tenanted by porcupines, a bear would occasionally take up his quarters, but he was sure to be observed and reported by the women who visited a well near the hill, and equally sure to be shot. During my stay at Chetterpur I killed two bears in this way, within a mile of the village.

Bears are often wounded and killed without making any show of resistance, but they sometimes prove very dangerous assailants, as the following example shows: Travelling one moonlight night in a palanquin between Aska and Berhampur, Mr. Minchin was roused by his bearers, who pointed out to him a bear among the bushes near the road; he had with him a single-barrelled rifle, with which he wounded the bear; it then disappeared over the raised bank of a tank close by, and Mr. Minchin loading again, approached the bank in hopes of another shot. Just as he mounted the bank the bear met him from the opposite side, and, rising on its hind legs, struck its claws with great force into his left breast just over the heart, knocking him backwards, after which, scared by the bearers, it made its escape. When the wound was examined the doctor declared that only the full development of the chest muscles had kept the claws from penetrating to the heart through the thin folds of the sleeping jacket.

But I myself shot, in some hills about five miles from Chetterpur, a bear which, with ample opportunity for mischief, showed abject cowardice.

In order to reduce the number of these beasts I one evening had a tent pitched near the hills, and went there with two companions to dine and sleep in order that before daylight we might get between the bears and their retreats, and intercept them as they left the gardens. We only fell in with one bear, which succeeded in reaching the hills without giving us a shot. We followed it to its den, but finding there was no chance of dislodging it, we turned towards the tents. Just then one of my peons pointed to a lofty and precipitous pinnacle, five hundred feet above us; there stood a bear motionless as a statue and watching our movements in front of the den. It was agreed that while the rest of the party watched the precipitous front of the rock I should climb up the back of the cone by an access which a sturdy villager offered to point out. It proved a difficult climb, and on reaching the top, which was perfectly flat, I found it completely covered, to a depth of three feet, by a network of the vine-like branches of some wild creeper, so tough and thick as to support my weight securely as I mounted the mass. In front of me on the other side of the rock, still in the same attitude, and still watching my comrades near the den, stood the bear about twenty paces off and with his back towards me. He still remained motionless and regardless of my presence, so I planted either foot securely on a sturdy branch and then whistled to attract his attention and get a side shot if possible. The bear simply looked over his shoulder at me, and then without stirring a foot resumed his watch. I brought matters to a crisis presently by sending a bullet through his loins; he uttered one wild yell and, instead of turning upon me, rushed forward and fell headlong over the precipice, at the foot of which we picked him up quite dead.

If the bear had charged me I feel sure my guide would have stood by me with his heavy staff. I could not have moved rapidly from my position on the branches of the creeper.

In the neighbourhood of Berhampur and Chetterpur jackals were extremely numerous, and instances of death from hydrophobia, occasioned by the bite of a mad jackal, several times occurred. One night a rabid beast made its way into the lines of the native regiment at Berhampur and bit five persons as they lay asleep in their open verandas. All these people died, and such cases were regarded as sure to be fatal.

I was therefore much alarmed when

my head servant awoke me one night and announced that three of the stable men and a valuable dog had been bitten by a mad jackal; he said he had heard of a Brahmin living in Ganjam who had treated many such cases successfully, and a messenger was sent in hot haste to summon him.

Excision or cautery of the bites seemed to me impossible owing to the position of the wounds. The first man attacked was seized by the great toe as he lay asleep in his hut, the jackal then rushed into the next hut where a horse-keeper, roused by the outcry, was just sitting up, and bit him in the upper part of the nose; from this hut the beast crossed the field to a cattle pen, but failed to get inside; returning, it ran into my stables and bit a poligar hound, and then seized a stable man by the tendons of the instep. At last one of the men threw a horse cloth over it, and it was beaten to death.

I shot the poor poligar dog in the morning, to avoid further risks; but when the Brahmin arrived with his remedy, he assured me that he could have saved the dog, as he would assuredly save the men, from hydrophobia.

The remedy, which he administered internally, betrayed itself both by its smell and its operation, and proved to consist mainly of the leaves of the datura, or stramonium plant, made into a pulp. The patients were warned to expect an attack of delirium and stupor, and were to eat nothing for twenty-four hours, when the effect of the medicine would pass away. The symptoms which the Brahmin led us to expect appeared and passed off in due course; they are those always produced by stramonium, and I have never entertained any doubt that this was the remedy used, though the Brahmin refused to make it known. Neither do I doubt that the jackal was mad, for these creatures never make such attacks under any other circumstances. Certain it is that none of the three men bitten had an attack of hydrophobia.

Datura seeds were formerly used by thieves in Tanjore in order to drug the food of travellers and rob them while insensible. A thief of this class would watch a traveller sit down to his bowl of rice, at one of the endowed chuttrums where a meal is provided for strangers, and sauntering up would sit down and engage him in friendly conversation, watching his opportunity to flick a few datura seeds, unobserved, among the rice, with which they were probably swallowed either unnoticed or passing for grains of the small pulse often sprinkled over curry and rice. Next day the traveller would recover from the effects of the stramonium to find that he had lost everything.

I sent an account of the episode of the jackal and the remedy used to *The Times*, but it was not inserted. I also wrote to an eminent London surgeon, detailing the facts of the case, but he replied that there was no proof the jackal was mad! I believe, however, that the claims of stramonium as a prophylactic to hydrophobia are not unknown to the profession, though it does not seem that any great confidence is placed in it. The case I have described ought to procure for it further attention and experiment. The Brahmin who treated my servants assured me that his remedy is efficacious even after hydrophobia has set in.

CHAPTER XIII.

MAHENDRA.

MAHENDRA GIRI, which means "Great India's Mountain," is entitled to special description, for on its summit, far from human abodes, and in positions difficult of access, are temples and carvings, the work of unknown hands at some unknown period. The Ooriyahs of the three ancient zemindaries which lie round the base of the mountain admit their ignorance on the subject; and though on one festal day in the year the mountain is visited, in virtue of some undefined title to reverence, no sect claims a right to its temples, nor is any act of worship performed in them.

The only legend I have heard which speaks of the sojourn of men in this solitude is derived, I believe, from the Mahábhárata, and says that the Pándava brothers, returning to Hastinapur from the south, were driven by their enemies to take refuge on this mountain for two years. Certain it is, however, that the ridge which forms the summit where the temples stand, rugged and narrow, and rising to a height of nearly five thousand feet, surrounded by forests and remote from any cultivated lands, would be a very untenable position for any body of men during a long period.

Yet on the very crest of the ridge, in a position where there is scarcely room to pitch a small tent, stands a shrine measuring about twelve feet square at its base, and about eighteen feet high, composed of fourteen blocks of hewn stone of cyclopean dimensions. There are three courses of four stones each; the lower blocks are about nine feet long and three feet cube, while the stones in the second and third courses diminish in length so as to contract the inner space as the building rises, and admit of it being closed at the top by a block of stone eight feet square by three feet thick, on the summit of which is placed a well-carved circular crown of about four feet in diameter. The blocks have been so adjusted as to give the sides the slight curve observable in the temples of Orissa, and borrowed, as I think, from the outline of the pine-apple.

How were these huge blocks handled and placed with nicety and precision in their places, on a narrow space rough with rocks? The task would be difficult and tedious even on level ground, and without the aid of mechanical appliances a multitude of men would be required. For these there is not standing room, and it is not strange that under such puzzling conditions the natives account for the building as the work of superhuman agents.

On the lower slopes of the ridge are

two other temples of rather larger size, but of the type of outline already indicated. They are built of small, finely carved stones fitted together without cement. There was formerly a fourth temple, but it has fallen into ruin. Not far off are a number of small semicircular grottos, built of rough flat stones piled so as to converge and form a dome like an oyster grotto; probably these dens afforded shelter to the workmen. In the wood hard by there is a spring of water capable of yielding an unfailing supply for their wants; it is the source of a stream which on its way to the plain falls over a precipice of some height.

Scattered about the hill-side lie blocks of stone, some of them partially hewn and some with tracings of bulls and other animals cut on them but left unfinished, suggesting work suddenly interrupted. The only other traces of human handiwork are two small spaces inclosed by rough stone walls. They are now occupied by stunted trees, almost the only ones which grow on the upper ridge, which runs for three or four miles from north to south; the base of the mountain extends over at least twenty miles, and its slopes are for the most part clothed with wood.

Such were the surroundings amongst which a party of us emerged about noon one day after an arduous climb of five or six hours through the woods on the eastern face of Mahendra.

Ever since it first became known to

me that in the centre of Ganjam there stood a mountain of ancient fame, the highest in that part of India, which had only once been ascended by an English officer (Major Strange, of the trigonometrical survey), I had made up my mind to visit Mahendra and see its ancient temples.

The Raja of Mundasá, one of the Ooriyah zemindars, whose estates included a portion of Mahendra, entered into these plans with enthusiasm, assisted materially in getting a tent and supplies carried up, and declared his intention of making his first ascent on the same occasion. It was not hard to assemble a few congenial spirits for such an expedition, and after many hours of toil, during which we scattered according to our respective physical powers, we looked in triumph from the summit across a thickly wooded country on to the white line of surf that marks the coast, and examined and wondered over the ancient carvings which had survived their history so many centuries.

Although great men in India are little used to physical exertion, the Raja of Mundasá carried out his resolution with great spirit; and when his litter broke down, he completed the ascent on foot, and bivouacked on the summit with his followers. Near the top, two young officers of our party overtook him, seated on a rock to rest; he made them sit beside him for awhile, and such conversation ensued as is possible between regimental Hindostani on the one part, and pure Ooriyah on the other. Observing the flushed cheeks and bedewed brows of his companions, the Raja courteously handed to them the pink check handkerchief to which he had himself been beholden. Put to the proof thus suddenly, they dealt with the kindly meant offer, gratefully of course, but differently, according to the presence of mind they respectively possessed, which in one case was great, and in the other very small!

That night several heavy showers fell, and, though we were sheltered from the rain, its effects reached us in an odd way. We had pitched the tent on a rocky slope, quite at the bottom of the upper ridge; and though no water entered from outside, there rose from a fissure in the rocky floor of the tent a jet of water six inches high, which obliged us to roll up our mattresses and shift as we could till daylight enabled us to move to a better site. Evidently some natural reservoir on the upper part of the ridge communicated with the rocky site we had chosen for the tent, and illustrated, much to our discomfort, the principle of the artesian well.

The zemindars and their people were much gratified by the appreciation shown for Mahendra, and great baskets of mandarin oranges and gallons of rich buffalo milk were brought up from all sides for our acceptance. The hamlets of the Sourah vassals of the neighbouring zemindars are built on the lowest slopes of the hill, and they herd their buffaloes wherever the coarse grass which these animals love is to be found; we saw their traces even on the lofty slope where our tent was pitched. The hills inhabited by the independent Sourahs rise full in view on the western side of Mahendra Giri to a height not far short of it. A very deep valley, which these people do not cross, separates them from the vassal Sourahs of Mundasá.

This visit to Mahendra Giri was followed at intervals by other expeditions, and in due time a substantial little cottage was built, at the cost of much toil and some failures, near one of the temples. It is now the property of the Mundasá Raja, who is careful to keep it in repair, and generously allows it to be occupied by such visitors as are induced to face the toil of the ascent, either by curiosity or in order to enjoy the delicious mountain climate. A letter written from the cottage by my old friend Mr. Minchin, who was one of our party on the occasion of the first ascent, reached me not long ago, and recalled its pleasant memories.

CHAPTER XIV.

THE KHOND HIGHLANDS.

HAD not the attention of the Government of India been drawn to the Khond highlands by the custom prevalent among the race of offering human victims to an imaginary being, known in their superstition as the Earth Goddess, the Khonds would probably have remained unnoticed and unvisited to this day. In seasons of drought it is their custom to propitiate the Earth Goddess by a sacrifice, and to restore fertility to the fields by burying here and there morsels of the flesh of the victim. A human sacrifice is held to be the most acceptable, but failing that a buffalo may be offered. The rite is known as the "Meria."

The Khonds never devoted a member of their own race to the "Meria"; the victims were kidnapped in childhood from the plains and sold to the Khonds by wretches of the lowest caste, who made this their trade. But the captives were not sacrificed then and there, nor were they made aware of their destiny; every indulgence available to the community was lavished upon them, and they were regarded as set apart for a sacred purpose. When the time came for a sacrifice, they were half stupefied with liquor and drugs, and taken to the appointed place in solemn procession, decorated with flowers. A heavy blow on the head from the club of the priest then put an end to the life of the victim, and the flesh cut into small pieces was distributed among the spectators, in order to be buried in their fields.

The disappearance of children from the villages in the plains was at last traced to professional kidnappers, and further inquiry brought to light the nature and object of their trade. The discovery was mainly due to Captain Macpherson, who has detailed in his published work on the subject many interesting particulars connected with the Khonds. He was charged by the supreme Government with the earliest operations directed towards the extinction of the practice of human sacrifice, and moving into the hills with a sepoy force rescued victims destined for the Meria from many Khond villages. But the Khonds collected in great numbers, and surrounding his force compelled him to give back the rescued victims.

After this unfortunate occurrence the Government organized a special agency for the accomplishment of their purpose. An irregular force of two or three hundred men was levied among the Ooriyah population, men inured to forest life and acquainted with the Khonds and their ways; they were suitably armed and equipped under intelligent native officers of their own class, and placed under the command of Colonel Campbell, assisted by his subordinate officer, Captain MacNeil.

Colonel Campbell was vested with special powers for dealing with the crime of human sacrifice, and furnished with an establishment of elephants and tents which enabled him to traverse every part of the Khond hills and to pass some months of every year in this way, visiting the strongholds of the superstition, rescuing intended victims, dispersing assemblages met for the purpose of human sacrifice, and endeavouring to engage the Khonds everywhere to substitute buffaloes for human victims. Steps were at the same time taken for putting an end to kidnapping, and so cutting off the supply of victims.

The special agency under Colonel Campbell, and subsequently under Captain MacNeil, who succeeded him, persevered for many years in the systematic efforts I have described to stamp out the practice of human sacrifice. And at the time of my arrival in Ganjam it was considered that this object had been attained, and the sacrifice of a buffalo everywhere substituted for that of a human being.

The persons rescued from time to time had now reached a considerable number, all dependent on the Government for the means of support. It was resolved to try and form an agricultural community of them; they were provided with lands, seed, cattle, and implements, and located in a village erected for them by the Government. It was hoped that the "Merias," as they had come to be called, would thus be able to support themselves; but the experiment was not a success. The little community consisted of persons bred up in idleness and trained to be helpless, and they continued helpless and dependent, their agriculture did not prosper, and they were never able to pay the trifling assessment which in the hope of stimulating their industry had been imposed upon their fields.

The special agency by the time its functions terminated had acquired much useful information, and had become intimately acquainted with the country inhabited by the Khonds, extending from the Mahanuddi on its northern border to the hills of the independent Sourahs behind Mahendra, and from the confines of Nagpore and Bustar in the west, to the line of ghauts overlooking the ancient Zemindaries of Goomsur and Soonda in Ganjam, which marked its eastern limits.

The officers of the trigonometrical survey had also explored this region, and added the record of its hills, valleys, and rivers to their admirable collection of maps. As the eastern face of the plateau is the highest part of the country, the rivers instead of flowing seaward follow a westerly course for some distance, and in the middle of the plateau sweep round, some to the north to join the Mahanuddi, and others to the south, falling into the river which debouches at Calingapatan.

The consequence of this formation is that the saucer-shaped valleys into which much of the country is divided are abundantly supplied with water, and rice is grown on their lower slopes without the aid of artificial sources of irrigation. The Khonds terrace these rice grounds with great care and skill, maintaining a perfectly horizontal surface. Their ploughing cattle are in part procured by barter from the low country, and partly of their own breeding.

A Khond got up for a journey to the Goomsur bazaars is a somewhat comical sight. His thick black hair is brought forward and rolled into a chignon on his forehead, and in it are sure to be sticking two or three half-smoked cheroots, his dusky skin shines with recent lubrication, and the white cloth folded round his waist is so disposed that its ends fall behind him like the tail of an ox. Across his shoulder is a lath of bamboo, at each end of which is a round bundle about the size of a man's head; this is his turmeric, which is neatly packed in leaves, and which he will barter in the bazaar for shining brass, ware, or cloth, or perhaps he will be seen on his return slowly urging up the ghaut some feeble, half-starved cow or bullock, which after a few months of the abundant fodder of the jungles will become sleek and fat. The picture, however, is incomplete without mention of the tungi and bow, both of which the Khond carries in his right hand, together with three or four arrows, headed with blades like dessert knives. This very truculent display, however, is only assumed on the principle "si velis pacem, para bellum." Probably his long-handled tungi has only been used to cut off the head of a goat, and his arrows are innocent of the taste of human blood.

The Khond feuds are conducted in keeping with this preference for the aspect of war over its stern realities. The race has become subdivided into septs and rival communities; something leads to a quarrel between two of them, and perhaps a life is taken, probably at a drinking bout, for the Khonds drink a great deal of "toddy," drawn from the sago palm, and distil a strong spirit from the flower of the mohwa tree; sometimes a whole village is drunk for days together. However, when once a man has been killed, his tribe feel bound to take a life in return, and at a convenient season a challenge is sent. A Khond herald mounts a hill overlooking the rival village, sounds a point of war on his horn, and shouts the challenge, naming time and place; usually a valley is selected on the sloping sides of which there are rocks and bushes affording convenient cover to both parties (they do not wish to see too much of each other). On the day of battle the opposing armies take up each its position (under cover), those who can afford it wear a sort of pinafore of thick buffalo hide, almost proof against an arrow, and some fix a pair of bison's horns on their heads, *terroris causâ*. On a sudden one party starts up and sends a flight of arrows across the valley, dropping under cover again at once. The enemy replies with a similar discharge. When no results follow upon prolonged fighting of this sort, a few braves on either side caper down into the bottom of the valley and a skirmish ensues which ought to lead to slaughter, but somehow this, too, often ends harmlessly, and so the war goes on for perhaps three weeks, until by some fortunate accident somebody is hit, and either the tribal honour is satisfied or a fresh score is incurred, to be settled on the next occasion.

After I took charge of the agency, intervention in these quarrels, and the suppression of female infanticide, which was still practised in some of the Khond communities, became the chief objects in view. The irregulars who had served under the former special agent were, for the most part, absorbed into the constabulary, which was at that time about being organized by the present Sir W. Robinson, then Inspector-General of Police; they retained their fire-arms, and bodies of them accompanied me when I visited the hills, under the command of an officer (Captain, now Major Lys) admirably qualified by temper and judgment for the duty of dealing with savages.

We located a few police-stations here

and there among the Khonds, with an organized system of patrol, and cases of the exposure of female infants were occasionally brought to light and punished with imprisonment or transportation. I found, however, that nothing but a severe and signal example would put an end to this practice, and on the occurrence of a flagrant case of immolation the perpetrator was hanged at the scene of the crime, after which cases ceased to be reported.

I was absent from Ganjam during the year 1865, and on my return, in January, 1866, the first news which met me as the steamer anchored was, "There is a 'row' in the Khond Hills, and a threatening of famine in Ganjam."

Both items of this unpleasant announcement were verified, and on reaching Ganjam I found my *locum tenens*, Mr. Thornhill, and the Inspector-General of Police in Goomsur, on the borders of the Khond Hills, with several junior officers.

Mr. (now Sir W.) Robinson and his lieutenants had just returned from the upper country, where our police had been in hostile collision with the Kootîya Khonds, in the western part of the country, a wilder and bolder tribe than their kinsmen on the borders of Goomsur. As our police posts were advanced, and the enforcement of a general control attempted, resentment and resistance were naturally aroused, and there followed encounters which did not pass off without bloodshed. The worst was over when I resumed charge, but the very next day came news of trouble nearer home.

There was to the south-west of Soorada a cluster of hills and valleys inhabited by some few hundred Khonds who bore a bad character, as having more debased habits than the rest of the nation. They owned a nominal allegiance to the Raja of Bodagudda, whose estate bordered the wild and rugged country they inhabited; it was separated from the Khond Hills on the Goomsur and Soorada side by an interval of some width, and which I find described in my diary as a beautiful level valley, with fine trees scattered about it, and along which we rode for twenty miles to the western corner of the triangular-shaped group of hills inhabited by these Khonds.

From this point I intended to enter their country and effect the capture of the murderers of the headman of an Ooriyah village on the Bodagudda border. This had been already attempted by a body of police, but they had been attacked by the Khonds and baffled. The people of the two villages to which the culprits belonged deserted their villages and took to less accessible refuges in their hills.

As most of our armed police were absent in the country of the Kootîya Khonds, I got together, with some difficulty, a body of about seventy constables, composed chiefly of men from the posts in the low country, and armed them with muskets. Two very efficient assistants were with me, and we made our way to a large village called Simli, lying just within the Khond border, and the people of which, being easily accessible, and having had no share in the disturbance, were on their good behaviour. Here we encamped; at night my enterprising lieutenants, Mr. Goodriche and Captain Pickance, made an attempt to surprise one of the retreats to which the rebels had withdrawn, and to which we had found a guide.

The expedition only led to the capture of two of the women and two little children, a result which in the sequel proved of far greater use to us than we could have supposed. Mr. Goodriche came back with a very wicked looking arrow sticking in the brim of his hat, but no other casualties occurred.

The next day our operations were wholly unlucky. I went out to visit the deserted villages, and endeavoured to find and communicate with some of their inhabitants; but one of my parties, owing to a mistake, became embroiled with the Khonds, who, without showing themselves, peppered them with their formidable arrows. I had to go with the rest of the men to extricate them, and we brought back with us two men severely wounded, my raw recruits having expended much powder and ball on rocks and trees, and greatly endangered the lives of their comrades and ourselves.

Degraded as these Khonds may be, and repulsive as is their appearance, it is to their credit that they have a great regard and respect for their women.

I visited our captives as they sat round their camp-fire in the morning, and found them bearing captivity with great philosophy; they only asked for tobacco and toddy in addition to their food. The tiny urchins, sitting with their toes in the warm ashes, had each a bit of a cigar in his mouth, and took kindly to the toddy, which we were assured was their daily regimen.

Their capture weighed more heavily on their relatives than on themselves, for next day the Mazi, or headman, sent me in a green bough and an arrow in token of submission, and proposed to come in for a parley. Several men and a few women appeared, the latter ugly hags, unclothed to the waist, with unkempt hair, and each with a pipe dangling from her mouth; but in spite of these personal drawbacks the ladies put in a word every now and then, and were listened to; and when the men hesitated to give up the murderers in exchange for the captives, the women urged acceptance with one voice, and carried their point. The murderers were surrendered, and certain articles of police equipment captured at the first collision were also given up; and when we marched across the country to Bodagudda the next day, our late enemies shouldered our baggage and carried it for us.

Before the conference closed however, an oath of renewed fealty to the Bodagudda Raja was sworn. The Raja had been afraid to accompany me, and his headman represented him. A bit of earth, a squirrel's skin, and a lizard were placed upon a tiger skin, together with a dagger, and the oath was pronounced over these symbols.

I brought back with me on one of my visits to the Khond Hills the seed pods of a tree which I have not seen elsewhere in India. It was about twenty feet high, with thick foliage, and if I remember right a rather small leaf; but its remarkable feature was the seed pod, which in some cases was between three and four feet long, with a breadth of four inches. Inside the pod were brown seeds like those of a horse chestnut, but larger and flatter. When the pod is dry it forms a formidable natural rattle, and when the wind sways the pods as they hang the effect may be imagined.

I sent my specimen to Kew Gardens, and found it on my last visit in the upper room of one of the museum houses there.

The forests in the Khond country, and at the base of the hills along the Ganjam border, consist mainly of sal trees. This is a very strong and durable wood, little inferior in value to teak. The trees rise straight and without a branch to a height of forty or fifty feet, after which the foliage spreads. They yield an excellent resin, called *dammer*, which is in general use throughout India.

In 1866, as the year wore on, the dark shadow of the Orissa famine spread and deepened over the northern half of Ganjam, bringing with it many a harrowing sight. During the greater part of the year my assistants * and I and the whole establishment were more or less occupied with the conduct of the various operations by which we endeavoured to combat the famine. Lord Napier, then Governor of Madras, visited the district, and gave his ready

* Messrs. Horsfall, Stewart, Goodriche, and Grigg, four University men, who had lately entered the Civil Service, were then assistants in Ganjam, and gave me their zealous aid in all that was done.

sanction to every feasible scheme of relief. The Ganjam and Chilka canal and other public works were undertaken, the poorest classes were fed at great relief houses, the weavers had a special contract given them for tent cloth for the commissariat, and the ryots, who in their poverty still shrank from attending the public food kitchens, were relieved by other special arrangements, and grants of seed grain were made to them.

When, in the course of the following year, my nine years' service in Ganjam came to an end, and I had to leave scenes and people for which I felt a warm regard, the period of suffering had ended, and prosperity had returned to the district.

THE CRY OF THE LAND.

OH, come, from all the winds desired, beloved,
Besought of dying Hope, delay no more,
Nor spurn the cry of sore extremity;
Delay no more!

Stoop low, ye dark-brow'd messengers of Heav'n,
Press your moist kiss upon the sleeping earth,
And wake the blessèd fragrance of the field—
The spell-bound field.

Cumber no more the full contented sea,
Nor fleet so fickle to the distant hills,
Nor stand with voiceless light'ning in the north:
Not so! Not so!

'Tis ill to dally thus with our dismay,
To us! to us! Ours be the hollow eyes,
The hearts that ache with watching of your ways,
To us! To us!

Ah! linger not, for it is ill with us.
Our little children take our heart away;
They kill us, these lean cheeks, these wasted hands—
These wasted hands.

There is no sound of water in the land,
  Upon the mere's dry bed the cattle die,
The voices fail from the deserted street ;
                    Shall all things fail ?

Higher than heav'n, hear Thou the desolate ;
  Command Thy clouds that they do visit us,
And bid Thine earth bring forth that we may live—
                    That we may live.

GANJAM, 1866.

NOTE.—Of the numerous orphans and deserted children left homeless during the famine, some were provided for in the Roman Catholic and Baptist Mission orphanages. Many others found an asylum in an orphanage instituted at Chetterpur by the Rev. Warner Ottley, M.A., chaplain of the district, entirely at his own expense, in a building purchased by him for the purpose. Here the orphans were maintained and educated till they grew up.